Your Happy Healthy Pet™

Puppy Care & Training
2nd Edition

GET MORE!
Visit www.wiley.com/
go/puppy_care

Bardi McLennan

Howell
Book House™

Howell Book House

Published by Wiley Publishing, Inc., Hoboken, New Jersey

For general information on our other products and services or to obtain technical support please contact our Customer Care Department within the U.S. at (800) 762-2974, outside the U.S. at (317) 572-3993 or fax (317) 572-4002.

Wiley also publishes its books in a variety of electronic formats. Some content that appears in print may not be available in electronic books. For more information about Wiley products, please visit our web site at www.wiley.com.

Library of Congress Cataloging-in-Publication Data:
McLennan, Bardi.
 Puppy care & training/Bardi McLennan.—2nd ed.
     p. cm.—(Your happy healthy pet)
 Includes index
 ISBN-13: 978-0-7645-8387-2 (alk: cloth)
 ISBN-10: 0-7645-8387-5 (alk: cloth)
 1. Puppies. 2. Puppies—Training. I. Title: Puppy care and training. II. Title. III. Series.
 SF427.M4735 2005
 636.7'07—dc22

10 9 8 7 6 5 4 3 2

Second Edition

Book design by Melissa Auciello-Brogan
Cover design by Michael J. Freeland
Book production by Wiley Publishing, Inc. Composition Services

About the Author

Bardi McLennan is the author of many books on dogs, including only the second complete history ever written about her own breed, the Welsh Terrier (*The Welsh Terrier Leads the Way*). She has written books on other breeds, including four since 2000 that have been published in Europe.

For fifteen years Bardi was a contributing editor to *Dog Fancy* magazine, and has written feature articles for the *AKC Gazette* and all major canine publications, as well as for many trade magazines in the pet industry. She has received the Kal Kan Pedigree Award for outstanding journalism on pet care, plus several awards from the Dog Writers Association of America, where she's been an active member since 1986.

No longer involved in breeding and showing her own dogs, Bardi has recently judged a Kerry Blue Terrier Sweepstakes and an Irish Terrier Sweepstakes.

About Howell Book House

Since 1961, Howell Book House has been America's premier publisher of pet books. We're dedicated to companion animals and the people who love them, and our books reflect that commitment. Our stable of authors—training experts, veterinarians, breeders, and other authorities—is second to none. And we've won more Maxwell Awards from the Dog Writers Association of America than any other publisher.

As we head toward the half-century mark, we're more committed than ever to providing new and innovative books, along with the classics our readers have grown to love. This year, we're launching several exciting new initiatives, including redesigning the Howell Book House logo and revamping our biggest pet series, Your Happy Healthy Pet™, with bold new covers and updated content. From bringing home a new puppy to competing in advanced equestrian events, Howell has the titles that keep animal lovers coming back again and again.

Contents

Shopping List

You'll need to do a bit of stocking up before you bring your new dog or puppy home. Below is a basic list of some must-have supplies. For more detailed information on the selection of each item below, and for specific guidance on what grooming tools you'll need, consult chapter 5.

- ☐ Food dish
- ☐ Water dish
- ☐ Dog food
- ☐ Leash
- ☐ Collar
- ☐ Crate

- ☐ Nail clippers
- ☐ Grooming tools
- ☐ Chew toys
- ☐ Toys
- ☐ ID tag

There are likely to be a few other items that you're dying to pick up before bringing your dog home. Use the following blanks to note any additional items you'll be shopping for.

- ☐ _____
- ☐ _____
- ☐ _____
- ☐ _____
- ☐ _____
- ☐ _____
- ☐ _____
- ☐ _____
- ☐ _____
- ☐ _____
- ☐ _____
- ☐ _____

Pet Sitter's Guide

We can be reached at (___)_____-_____ Cellphone (___)_____-_____

We will return on _____ (date) at _____ (approximate time)

Dog's Name _____

Breed, Age, and Sex _____

Important Names and Numbers

Vet's Name _____ Phone (___)_____- _____

Address_____

Emergency Vet Name _____ Phone (___)_____- _____

Address_____

Poison Control _____ (or call vet first)

Other individual to contact in case of emergency _____

_____

Puppy's Routine

Wake up _____ a.m. Outside to potty area.

Food & water _____a.m. Outside to play, go potty.

Confinement in _____ from _____ to _____ Outside to play, go potty.

Lunch & fresh water _____ p.m. Outside to play, go potty.

Confinement in _____ from _____ to _____ Outside to play, go potty.

Dinner & fresh water _____ p.m. Outside to play, go potty.

Remove water bowl. Outside before bedtime _____ p.m.

Bedtime in crate with a biscuit at _____ p.m.

Food amounts and type of food for each meal: _____

_____

Medications needed (dosage and schedule) _____

Any special medical conditions _____

Grooming instructions _____

My dog's favorite playtime activities, quirks, and other tips_____

_____

_____

Part I
Welcoming a Puppy

The Puppy

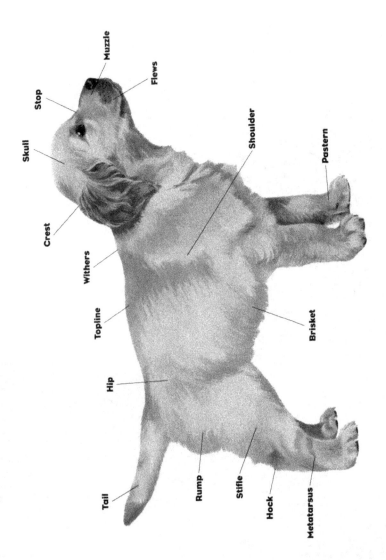

Chapter 1

Congratulations on Your New Puppy!

Puppies arrive in their new homes with an abundance of charm, and they all seem to come into the world knowing exactly how to use it to beguile their new owners. They have all kinds of wonderful characteristics, some of which are the very reasons you chose the pup you did—playful exuberance, a sweet face, and a soft, warm body to cuddle. In fact, being taken in by your puppy's charisma may just be what marks the start of a lifelong friendship. The memories of naughtiness fade, but the charm remains.

Puppies also come "complete with batteries," and are ready to absorb their environment like a sponge. A pup learns from every gesture of your arms, legs, face; from your tone of voice; from how you speak to others and how differently you speak to him. Your puppy has an inner clock that quickly resets to his new household's routine—when to wake up, when to eat, when Johnny leaves for school, when to go to sleep. Everything. And he learns it all in a matter of days!

What you teach, *how* you teach, and *when* you teach will determine what kind of adult your puppy will become. If everyone in the household races to answer the phone, one ding-a-ling will be the starter's gun for the puppy, too. On the other hand, you can (and should) teach your puppy to sit and stay when you are on the phone.

Note I used the word "teach" rather than "train." Teaching allows your puppy to participate in the learning process. You teach and the pup learns. Training is essentially robotic. Soldiers are trained. Circus animals are trained. It's the "don't think, just obey" method, and it should not be used on puppies. A year from now, if you're considering competitive obedience, you may decide to go that route, which is okay because by then your puppy will have *learned* how to understand your instructions.

The puppy has so much to learn that he may become sloppy about house rules, only because he is in such a hurry to know it all. It is your responsibility (in addition to basic care) to maintain consistency in enforcing the rules and disciplining your puppy. And by "discipline" I mean positive *teaching*, not punishment. Each person in the family needs to know and use the same "action" words (sit, come, off, etc.) in the same tone of voice, and require the same outcome, or else the puppy will be confused. Teaching your puppy is truly not complicated, and I'll go into it in detail later in this book.

Puppies, like these Siberian Huskies, have a lot to learn. It's your job to be their loving teacher.

Preparing for Your Puppy

There are a few things that should have been taken care of before you brought the puppy home, but it's not too late to do them *today!*

The first is to locate a veterinarian (your pup's second-best friend). You can often get a referral from your pup's breeder or from friends, relatives, or neighbors who take good care of their dogs. Call the veterinarian to make a get-acquainted appointment. In some areas vets are overloaded and can't take on new patients, and you may have to ask for yet another referral. Do not be intimidated. If you do not care for the doctor's manner, personality, office personnel, or anything else, *change vets!*

Call your local canine control officer or town official to find out at what age your puppy will require a license and what other local laws apply to dogs in your town. A license tag and proof of a rabies vaccination is usually required for dogs 6 months of age or over. That tag, along with an ID tag, should be worn on the dog's regular collar (not the training collar) for identification. Many towns now have leash laws, for example, that require your dog to be leashed whenever he is out in public. Many also require you to pick up after your dog. Ignorance of local ordinances can result in stiff fines.

There's a lot to do to get ready for a new puppy like this Australian Shepherd.

What Is the AKC?

The American Kennel Club (AKC) is the oldest and largest pure-bred dog registry in the United States. Its main function is to record the pedigrees of dogs of the breeds it recognizes. While AKC registration papers are a guarantee that a dog is pure-bred, they are absolutely not a guarantee of the quality of the dog—as the AKC itself will tell you.

The AKC makes the rules for all the canine sporting events it sanctions and approves judges for those events. It is also involved in various public education programs and legislative efforts regarding dog ownership. More recently, the AKC has helped establish a foundation to study canine health issues and a program to register microchip numbers for companion animal owners. The AKC has no individual members—its members are national and local breed clubs and clubs dedicated to various competitive sports.

Identifying Your Dog

It's a terrible thing to think about, but your dog could somehow, someday, get lost or stolen. How would you get him back? Your best bet is to have some form of identification on your dog. You can choose from a collar and tags, a tattoo, a microchip, or a combination of these.

Every dog should wear a buckle collar with identification tags. They are the quickest and easiest way for a stranger to identify your dog. It's best to inscribe the tags with your name and phone number; you don't need to include your dog's name.

But tags can fall off or can be taken off, and as they age they can also become illegible. There are two ways to permanently identify your dog. The first is a tattoo, placed on the inside of your dog's thigh. The tattoo should be your social security number or your dog's AKC registration number. The Canadian Kennel Club requires all dogs to be tattooed with the breeder's registration number. The problem with tattoos, though, is that wherever you choose to tattoo the dog (usually it is done in the inner thigh), you must always keep that area free of hair or the tattoo will not be visible.

The second form of permanent ID is a microchip, a tiny transponder, about the size of a grain of rice, encased in sterile glass. It is placed under the skin of your dog's shoulder by the veterinarian and remains there forever. Each chip has a unique number. When a microchip reader (not used by most canine control officers in animal shelters) is passed over the transponder, it reads the chip's number. Microchips are becoming more and more popular and are certainly the wave of the future.

A microchip or a tattoo number is useless by itself, though, which is why you must register the number with a microchip recovery service. The American Kennel Club has one, called the Companion Animal Recovery (CAR) program, or Home Again. When you register with any service, the number is stored in a database with your contact information and pertinent information about the dog. The information will also include your veterinarian's name and phone number along with a contact you designate if you are unreachable.

You'll also need to do some shopping for your puppy, and I'll talk about that in chapter 2. But if you haven't already taken care of the things mentioned in this chapter, put them at the top of your "must do" list for tomorrow.

Chapter 2

What Your New Puppy Needs

What your new puppy needs most is *you*—a responsible person to be at home while your silly girl is learning what she can and can't do. If no one is home to take on this job, the pup has no choice but to teach herself. Puppies are extremely quick to learn, and that is exactly how puppy problems begin. Left to make her own decisions as to what she can or can't do will only get her in trouble.

A puppy looks at the world in a very simple way: If she is able to do it, it must be okay. So she *will do* things like pull down the curtains, chew the rug, spread the trash all over the floor, and other activities you probably will not like as she discovers she is *able* to and no one is around to prevent her mistakes. Puppies should not be punished for these normal (though unacceptable) canine behaviors, because it is you who are at fault for not preventing them.

So choose a good time to bring the new puppy home—when whoever is in charge of teaching the pup her first lessons in acceptable family manners is home most of the day. The beginning of a vacation period is a good choice if you work.

There are also lots of other things your pup needs. The box on page 19 is a little shopping list for you. But let's look at some of those items in more detail.

Food and Water Bowls

Your puppy needs a sturdy food dish and a separate water bowl. A mat to put them on is not just for decoration—it will save your floor from slurped water and spilled food. If your pup has long, hanging ears, get dishes specially made to keep those ears out of her food and water. (They save you from having to clean ears twenty times a day and mop the kitchen when she shakes her head.) Consider bowls with weighted bases or non-slip bottoms so your dog can't push them all around the room. A raised stand to hold the bowls will keep food and water where they belong and at a comfortable height.

Lightweight plastic bowls are not a good idea for a teething, chewing puppy. Besides, they are too easily tipped over. If your puppy is in an exercise pen, you can get a water bowl that hangs on the wire and can be raised as the pup grows.

Food

Begin with whatever puppy food the breeder was feeding, ask your veterinarian, or buy a top-quality food made especially for puppies. Veterinarians today agree it is not necessary to add vitamins or minerals to a quality dog food for a healthy puppy. Too many vitamins (especially for large breeds) are actually detrimental.

Don't forget the treats! Small, plain dog biscuits are fine for "good puppy" rewards and an occasional treat. Fancy flavored treats are okay for adult dogs, but young puppies do better on a blander diet—and fewer treats! (You'll find detailed information on feeding in chapter 5.)

Sturdy, separate food and water bowls are essentials for any dog. This is a Boston Terrier.

Collar and Leash

Dog collars and leashes today are not merely utilitarian. They are definitely high fashion, and you'll find them in every imaginable color, with patterns of flowers, stripes, or prints, with or without rhinestones or studs, in a variety of fabrics as well as the old standby, rolled or braided leather. Before you go overboard, remember that your puppy may go through as many as six different collar sizes as she grows, and any designer item you choose today will probably have to be replaced over those first eighteen months as the pup's personality or size changes, or your own whims do.

It is very sad to see a little puppy weighed down with a heavy chain collar and a leash strong enough to restrain a cow! Be sure each collar and leash you select matches the current size and strength of your puppy. (What else they match is up to your mood of the moment.) Take your dog with you to the pet supply store to be sure you get the right size collar, and just keep in mind that you'll probably be back in a couple of months for a bigger one! The leash will last longer. Unless, of course, the dog is allowed to use it as a teething toy—definitely *not* a recommended game.

Warning: A training (or "choke") collar should *never* be left on a dog, and especially not on a puppy. Collars that can tighten around the dog's neck are meant to be used only as training devices and must be removed when the lesson is over. They are not intended for continuous wear because they are dangerous. If this type of collar catches on any object, the dog can easily strangle in her efforts to get free. Stick with soft buckle- or snap-closure collars for everyday wear. If you opt for motivational training, you'll be staying with the soft collar.

Picker-Uppers

Dog waste has to be disposed of, and there are several easy ways to do it. Pooper scoopers are easy-to-use clean-up tools, and backyard waste systems (that work with natural enzymes) are a popular means of disposal.

More and more towns are enforcing ordinances requiring owners to pick up after their dogs in all public areas. All responsible dog owners today carry disposable plastic mitts or plastic bags—a must when you take your dog anywhere outside that is off your property. You put your hand in the bag or mitt, pick up the excrement, fold the plastic down over your hand, and carry it home or to the nearest trash bin.

Puppy Essentials

You'll need to go shopping *before* you bring your puppy home. There are many, many adorable and tempting items at pet supply stores, but these are the basics.

- **Food and water dishes.** Look for bowls that are wide and low or weighted in the bottom so they will be harder to tip over. Stainless steel bowls are a good choice because they are easy to clean (plastic never gets completely clean) and almost impossible to break. Avoid bowls that place the food and water side by side in one unit—it's too easy for your dog to get his water dirty that way.
- **Leash.** A six-foot leather leash will be easy on your hands and very strong.
- **Collar.** Start with a nylon buckle collar. For a perfect fit, you should be able to insert two fingers between the collar and your pup's neck. Your dog will need larger collars as she grows up.
- **Crate.** Choose a sturdy crate that is easy to clean and large enough for your puppy to stand up, turn around, and lie down in.
- **Nail cutters.** Get a good, sharp pair that are the appropriate size for the nails you will be cutting. Your dog's breeder or veterinarian can give you some guidance here.
- **Grooming tools.** Different kinds of dogs need different kinds of grooming tools. See chapter 5 for advice on what to buy.
- **Chew toys.** Dogs *must* chew, especially puppies. Make sure you get things that won't break or crumble off in little bits, which the dog can choke on. Very hard plastic bones are a good choice. Dogs love rawhide bones, too, but pieces of the rawhide can get caught in your dog's throat, so they should only be allowed when you are there to supervise.
- **Toys.** Watch for sharp edges and unsafe items such as plastic eyes that can be swallowed. Many toys come with squeakers, which dogs can also tear out and swallow. All dogs will eventually destroy their toys; as each toy is torn apart, replace it with a new one.

Grooming Tools

Your new puppy needs to be groomed at least once or twice a week. Even the hairless Chinese Crested needs special attention (sunblock, for one thing!). There are special brushes and combs for every type of coat. Most puppies will shed their puppy coat as the adult one grows in. This shedding causes mats (clumps of hopelessly tangled hair) in longhaired dogs—and speckled furniture and people's clothing from shorthaired dogs. Definitely, your dog needs a brush!

She will also need to have her nails clipped. There are two types of nail trimmers: one uses a scissors action, the other is grimly referred to as a guillotine clipper. Choose whichever one you find comfortable to handle. Either one does the job. (The "how to" about using these tools comes in chapter 5.)

Toys

The most important item on your shopping list, at least according to your dog, is an assortment of appropriate toys—appropriate for her size, age, and personal preferences. Safe, fun, interactive doggy toys abound. If your new puppy is your "only child," you'll be tempted to buy one of each. When you come home with a shopping bag full, give the puppy just one or two, possibly add a third later, and save the rest for another day. Variety is the spice of life, and that also applies to dog toys. Every few days, you can add a new one and subtract an oldie, but always let the favorite toy remain as puppy's "security blanket."

Shopping for puppy toys is always fun. These Lhasa Apsos are enjoying their assortment.

One good interactive toy is the red, hard rubber, beehive-shaped Kong that bounces erratically when dropped. The pup will soon learn to drop it and make it bounce by herself. There are several shapes and sizes, including ones made so that tiny treats can be stuffed inside—making it a good toy for a home-alone pup.

Some balls are meant to be thrown and retrieved. Others, like a large soccer-size ball, can be pushed, hit, and nosed by the pup alone. A ball with a bell inside maintains a puppy's interest in the game. Rope toys are great for solitary chewing and for *mild, controlled* tug-of-war (held down at the level of the dog's head). Rawhides offer hours of chewing, and so are more occupational than playful. Plush dinosaurs, hedgehogs, and numerous other characters produce sounds that range from squeaks to roars. Have fun!

Watch your puppy when she's playing with chew toys, because not every toy is safe for every dog. Some dogs confuse the concept of "play" with "destroy" and are interested only in terminating whatever you buy. Stick with toys that require your participation, or, for solitary play, the larger-size hard rubber toys and balls.

Keeping Puppy Confined

You will need something called an exercise pen, or ex-pen (read: *playpen*), if your puppy cannot be confined to the kitchen or other safe area using a baby gate. The ex-pen will keep your puppy safe and in one place, but it also gives her room to play and access to water, and enables her to see what's going on around her and to use newspapers if she's a latchkey pet with no one home during the day to take her outside. Do not enclose your pup behind a solid door, because that isolates her from your family and is like banishment.

You'll find good old baby gates sold in pet supply stores as "pet gates." Choose one that fits your doorway securely, is high enough that the pup can't easily jump over it, and is constructed so the pup won't be encouraged to try her climbing techniques. Some are irresistibly chewable, but not if they are first sprayed with a taste deterrent such as Bitter Apple.

You'll also need to keep your puppy confined while she's in the car, so she doesn't plop herself into your lap or try to slither under your feet while you are driving. The canine seat belt is the latest car safety feature, and is a worthwhile investment if you don't have room in your car for a crate. (*Never leave any dog in any car in warm weather for any length of time.* Heatstroke is rapid and fatal.) When your puppy is older, a back-seat barrier will keep a large dog safely in the back seat of a car or in the rear of an SUV or station wagon.

Crate and/or Bed

Your puppy needs a crate. It is a puppy's bed of choice, a private, personal, snug den where your dog can sleep, chew a toy, and watch the world around her, completely undisturbed. (This is an important aspect of your puppy's life, and chapter 4 has more information on using the crate.)

Crates come in two styles: closed (fiberglass) or open (wire)—each type has pluses and minuses. The closed crate is draft-proof and more portable, but some pups (and their owners) want to be able to see more of the world around them. The open variety offers this visibility, but most dogs like their open crate to be covered at bedtime. It is also difficult to transport when it is set up. Either type must be placed away from drafts and sources of heat or air-conditioning.

Regardless of which style you decide on, it's important to get the correct size. This is not a puppy playroom or a canine condo. It is basically a bed, and the pup will curl up in about one-third of the space. Consider the adult size of your pup and get a crate that will allow her to stand up, turn around, and lie down. A bigger crate will enable your puppy to soil in the crate and then get far away from it—exactly what you don't want, because you will be using the crate as a housetraining tool. If the right size crate gives her more space than she needs for the next couple of months, add an adjustable barrier to block off part of the

This Cavalier King Charles Spaniel has a safe, warm place to snuggle in for a nap.

back of the crate; as the pup grows, it can be removed. For large breeds, it may be wiser to have a crate size suitable for a puppy up to 6 months of age, and then get another adult-size crate that will last the dog a lifetime. (Some breeders will lend you a puppy crate. Check it out.)

The best bedding in the crate is a folded bath towel. It's washable or disposable—accidents happen in the best of homes. If you want a fancy, cuddly doggy bed for your adorable puppy, fine, but in the beginning use it just for occasional (supervised) naps in the family room, not while housetraining or for overnight. Puppies teethe, and so they chew on everything. Dog beds are no exception.

What *You* Will Need

All of the items I have mentioned in this chapter are available at your local pet supply store or through pet supply catalogues and Web sites. There are also some things you, as the owner of a new puppy, will need: a good veterinarian; books and instructional videos about your chosen breed (or dogs in general); the names of a dog trainer who teaches puppy kindergarten classes, a professional pet sitter, an accredited boarding kennel, and a highly recommended groomer.

Puppies, like this Australian Shepherd, can make you crazy. You'll need to keep your sense of humor!

If you have a backyard, you also need a fence. The style can be geared to your home, but you definitely must consider what will be safe and secure, given the dog's adult size and temperament. If full fencing is not possible, consider a dog run for those dark and stormy nights and crack-of-dawn days when the dog *has* to go out and you'd rather be indoors. Free-standing dog runs are available that can be dismantled and taken along with you if you move. It won't take the place of the daily walks and playtime needed for healthy physical and mental exercise, but it is a great convenience.

What else will you need to handle your new puppy? Patience and a sense of humor. Make sure you have plenty of both!

Chapter 3

Puppy-Proofing Your Home

Making your home safe for a new puppy will require the same careful preparations you would need for a toddler—in some cases, more! For example, a toddler might play with a plastic bottle full of a harmful chemical for several minutes before trying to unscrew the top. Extremely dangerous, but a puppy (without benefit of hands) can easily puncture the container with sharp, needle-like teeth, making the danger instantaneous.

A toddler may empty the garbage can all over the floor, but you can tell her that trash cans are off-limits and she won't be doing it over and over and over again. A puppy smells chicken bones that are in the trash today, tomorrow the enticement is cheese, and the next day hamburger. The association is different each time, and it is not obvious to the puppy that it is the *container* that's off limits.

Teach by prevention! In the case above, get trash cans with tight-fitting lids and put them away where your puppy can't reach them. If you catch him in the act of rummaging, use a guttural *"accht!"* instead of "no." It will sound more like the warning growl from the pup's mother.

The box on page 26 is a puppy-proofing checklist you can use to remind everyone in the family of how to keep the puppy, and all your worldly goods, safe. In addition, here are some things you need to think about as you get your home ready for your new puppy. Remember to treat your new puppy like a toddler and be thankful that he will learn acceptable behavior in a matter of months, or almost as quickly as you can teach him.

Puppy-Proofing Your Home

You can prevent much of the destruction puppies can cause and keep your new dog safe by looking at your home and yard from a dog's point of view. Get down on all fours and look around. Do you see loose electrical wires, cords dangling from the blinds, or chewy shoes on the floor? Your pup will see them, too!

In the kitchen:

- Put all knives and other utensils away in drawers.
- Get a trash can with a tight-fitting lid.
- Put all household cleaners in cupboards that close securely; consider using childproof latches on the cabinet doors.

In the bathroom:

- Keep all household cleaners, medicines, vitamins, shampoos, bath products, perfumes, makeup, nail polish remover, and other personal products in cupboards that close securely; consider using childproof latches on the cabinet doors.
- Get a trash can with a tight-fitting lid.
- Don't use toilet bowl cleaners that release chemicals into the bowl every time you flush.
- Keep the toilet bowl lid down.
- Throw away potpourri and any solid air fresheners.

In the bedroom:

- Securely put away all potentially dangerous items, including medicines and medicine containers, vitamins and supplements, perfumes, and makeup.
- Put all your jewelry, barrettes, and hairpins in secure boxes.
- Pick up all socks, shoes, and other chewables.

In the rest of the house:

- Tape up or cover electrical cords; consider childproof covers for unused outlets.
- Knot or tie up any dangling cords from curtains, blinds, and the telephone.

- Securely put away all potentially dangerous items, including medicines and medicine containers, vitamins and supplements, cigarettes, cigars, pipes and pipe tobacco, pens, pencils, felt-tip markers, craft and sewing supplies, and laundry products.
- Put all houseplants out of reach.
- Move breakable items off low tables and shelves.
- Pick up all chewable items, including television and electronics remote controls, cellphones, shoes, socks, slippers and sandals, food, dishes, cups and utensils, toys, books and magazines, and anything else that can be chewed on.

In the garage:

- Store all gardening supplies and pool chemicals out of reach of the dog.
- Store all antifreeze, oil, and other car fluids securely, and clean up any spills by hosing them down for at least ten minutes.
- Put all dangerous substances on high shelves or in cupboards that close securely; consider using childproof latches on the cabinet doors.
- Pick up and put away all tools.
- Sweep the floor for nails and other small, sharp items.

In the yard:

- Put the gardening tools away after each use.
- Make sure the kids put away their toys when they're finished playing.
- Keep the pool covered or otherwise restrict your pup's access to it when you're not there to supervise.
- Secure the cords on backyard lights and other appliances.
- Inspect your fence thoroughly. If there are any gaps or holes in the fence, fix them.
- Make sure you have no toxic plants in the garden.

Keep Things Out of Reach

Begin with all the obvious precautions. Put all solvents, chemicals, medications, and similar items out of reach. That means anything you consider potentially harmful, from mild to wild. That also means such items must be stored higher than the full-grown dog can jump, or behind cupboard doors that cannot be pried open. Paws and noses are incredibly adept at opening almost anything that's closed! The plastic catches sold to keep toddlers out of kitchen cabinets and other storage places work well for dogs, too. Spray the catches with a taste deterrent such as Bitter Apple so they can't be manipulated by prying teeth.

Now is the time to read product labels. If there's a poison warning on any container, be sure everyone in the household knows it and stash the item on a high shelf in the garage or another safe place. Prescription medicines are not the only ones to be guarded. All over-the-counter medications should also be kept behind closed doors. You probably don't consider things you use every day for personal hygiene to be dangerous, but mouthwash, toothpaste, soap, deodorants, and similar products are poisonous to puppies. Put them away, and be sure to discard the empty containers where the dog can't get at them.

Anything that is within reach, a puppy will chew on—as this Samoyed demonstrates.

Granted, you can't hide everything you own or live in an empty shell. But to avoid disaster there are two things you can do. First, *be aware* of dangers and of where your pup is and what he is doing. Second, *confine* your puppy whenever you can't keep an eye on him. In other words, use the crate and use pet gates.

Putting dangerous items out of reach and limiting your puppy's unsupervised access to certain rooms are simple ways to make your job of teaching easier. If all those things are lying around in easy reach, you'll be saying "no!" a thousand times a day—and what little puppy wants to hear that?

By puppy-proofing your home, you remove the dangers and can proceed with positive training. Rufus will get smiles and praise and quickly learn what he needs to do to earn them. The occasional, necessary "no!" will then have powerful meaning.

Knick-Knacks

Puppies have no idea of the material value of things, and it's strange how few people realize this until it's too late. Put your precious china ornaments up high (or away) if a long tail might wipe them off the coffee table. Remove the Persian rug if it's in a hallway where you won't see it being chewed or urinated on. Lift up out of reach (or disconnect) lamp cords and television and radio wires that could be chewed and appliances that could be pulled down by your dog when you're on the phone or in the shower. Fold back the ends of runners and table-cloths that hang over the edge of the table, ready to be yanked in the blink of an eye.

Indoors and Outdoors

Protect your puppy from every outside door that does not lead to a safely fenced-in yard. All it takes is for the door to be opened a crack, and the pup can slip through to become another lost dog statistic. Outside, check gates and mend your fences—constantly!

To protect growing muscles, joints, and bones, keep the puppy on flooring where he has traction. Slippery floors can cause all kinds of permanent damage to growing pups.

This Labrador Retriever found a great treasure in the backyard. But if that boot has been in contact with anything toxic, it's a danger to puppies.

Toxic Plants

Attractive, innocent-looking plants that you've probably nursed along for years may be poisonous to dogs—particularly puppies, who are in the business of using *all* their senses, including taste.

Some of the common houseplants that are poisonous include ivy, dieffenbachia (also called dumbcane), poinsettia, Jerusalem cherry, and philodendron. Once you get outdoors, the list gets a lot longer, from all bulbs (not necessarily the plant, just the bulb and root system), including daffodils, lilies, and tulips, to many flowering shrubs and trees. Among the common garden plants that are especially harmful to puppies (and can be fatal) are foxglove, chrysanthemum leaves, larkspur, ivy, yew, holly, hydrangea, azalea, and many of the wild berry-bearing plants, such as elderberry and chokecherry. Mushrooms of every kind, including toadstools, can be fatal.

This warning is not meant to terrify you, but only to inform you so you'll take another look at your garden (indoors and out). As an added precaution against any plants you are not sure about, or ones you value and don't want chewed or dug up, there are several products on the market that keep animals away from your plants. Some claim they can remove yellowing or urine burn from the lawn. Some of these products may not be safe for your puppy, though. Check with your vet first, before you buy, to be sure.

Watch closely what your puppy is doing while you are weeding the garden. *Teach* him the boundaries of your garden by walking him around it on a leash (so you have instant control to prevent a misstep). This lesson, by the way, in no way guarantees that your puppy now or two years from now will walk sedately down the garden path while the squirrel he's pursuing dashes through the flower bed! Even the Father of our Country took down a cherry tree in a weak moment.

Here's one easy way to keep your pup away from large potted houseplants: Put aluminum foil around the pot, extending up to cover the lower foliage. Then take the added precaution of spraying the foil and any exposed leaves with Bitter Apple Plant and Leaf Protector.

Is your garden safe for your pup? All plants, indoors and out, are liable to be tasted.

Other Poisons

Some of the most dangerous poisons are found in the garage: gardening aids such as pesticides and fertilizers, and the number-one killer of pets, antifreeze—a mere teaspoon of which, licked off the garage floor, can be fatal.

If your dog vomits up any poison he has ingested, including plant parts, it is extremely important to save it for identification so your vet can decide on the best course of treatment. (Use a plastic clean-up bag or put any plastic bag over your hand, pick up the material, and turn the bag down over it.)

Being armed with the evidence is one thing, but if you even suspect the pup has ingested a foreign substance, what you do next could save his life. The best thing to do is contact the ASPCA Animal Poison Control Center (see the box below).

ASPCA Animal Poison Control Center

The ASPCA Animal Poison Control Center has a staff of licensed veterinarians and board-certified toxicologists available 24 hours a day, 365 days a year. The number to call is (888) 426-4435. You will be charged a consultation fee of $50 per case, charged to most major credit cards. There is no charge for follow-up calls in critical cases. At your request, they will also contact your veterinarian. Specific treatment and information can be provided via fax. Put the number in large, legible print with your other emergency telephone numbers. Be prepared to give your name, address, and phone number; what your puppy has gotten into (the amount and how long ago); your puppy's breed, age, sex, and weight; and what signs and symptoms the puppy is showing. You can log onto www.aspca.org and click on "Animal Poison Control Center" for more information, including a list of toxic and nontoxic plants.

Other Small Creatures

Your kids have a couple of hamsters—so what precautions are in order? Several, but they all boil down to one thing: *separation*. No matter how sweet, dear, and adorable little Rufus may be, he is first and foremost a dog. And dogs are not inclined to leave alone little creatures such as mice, gerbils, and hamsters. "Chase" is the name of the game, and "catch" is the sad end of it.

Be very sure the kids understand that their other pets must never (*never!*) be out of their cages if the puppy is in the room or can push his way into the room. Despite magazine pictures you see to the contrary, these species do not instinctively mix socially. (Those photos are carefully posed using highly trained animals handled by exceptional trainers!)

Cats

Cats and kittens can be carefully introduced to dogs (preferably older cats to puppies, kittens to adult dogs), and even after a rocky start, most will settle down. They will either become bosom buddies or a love-hate relationship will keep them forever at a safe distance. Their owners learn to live with it.

Puppies can make a mess out of anything—as this Old English Sheepdog demonstrates. All you can do is clean up and laugh.

Introduce the two by leaving the pup in his crate to allow the cat time to investigate. When that goes off without too much hissing or barking, hold the puppy in your lap and let the cat proceed with feline caution. Do *not* hold the kitty or you could be scratched to shreds! Be careful, too, that the pup doesn't get scratched around the eyes or face. (Wash the area immediately and thoroughly if this happens.)

Generally the cat will run off (or more accurately, run *up*) to where she feels safe, leaving the puppy deprived of the chase. If so, good. Puppy has learned that cats play by different rules.

It's a myth that cats and dogs can't be friends. Proper introductions and supervised interaction is essential, though.

Chapter 4

Starting Off Right

Begin as you mean to continue. Bring the puppy into the house and give her a complete tour *on a loose leash*. This is the pup's first introduction to whatever limitations you want to put on her future access to your possessions—your furniture, golf clubs, books, the kids' toy shelves, and so on.

This is not the right time for "no." (The puppy might begin to think that "no" is her name!) Instead, warn her away from untouchables by using a guttural *"aacht!"* combined with a very slight tug-and-release of the leash *as* she sniffs. She's new at this, and just saying "puppy!" (or her name) in a happy voice may be enough to get her to look at you—and stop what she's doing. "Good dog." Back to happy chatter as you move on.

All you are doing is letting her know (using a growl sound she understands) what things she will have to avoid in the future. Let her sniff first, because she'll remember the objects more by scent than by sight. Then she looks up at you and is praised. Think of it this way: "No!" means "Don't *do* that!" whereas *"aacht!"* means "Don't even *think* of doing it!"

Chit-chat is natural and pleasurable to both of you, but in the beginning let the puppy learn her name because everyone is using it in connection with things she finds pleasurable—play, food, and praise. The human-canine teaching language is based on short, simple words that are consistently applied to specific actions *as* those actions take place. One second later is too late. The connection is lost. If you use the word "din-din" many times while fixing her meals, that word will stand out in the midst of a five-minute speech on nutrition as a clue to the observant pup that she's about to eat.

TIP

Puppy Underfoot

Young puppies are quick, clumsy, and curious, and they can get underfoot in a flash. While there is an obvious difference in size between a 10-week-old Labrador Retriever and a Chihuahua of the same age, their mental development is about the same. One difference is the smaller the puppy, the greater her need for physical protection. Watch it! The puppy is bonding to you, so she'll stay as close to you as she can get—in front of, beside, or behind you, or lying across your feet so you won't leave without her. Watch out, too, for tails that can get caught in doors, and human failings such as a show of impatience or anger in your face or voice. Young puppies are supersensitive to every kind of hurt.

This first guided tour teaches your puppy the layout of her new home, what it looks like, smells like, even feels like (rugs, carpets, tile, wood), and that some things are off limits even to adorable puppies. There is one more important lesson she is learning from this adventure: that *you* are her new leader, the He- or She-Who-Must-Be-Obeyed. If you do not take on this role, the puppy will. Somebody's got to do it, and she'll fill the vacancy immediately! You may be familiar with the saying "Lead, follow, or get out of my way." Every dog is born knowing it and lives her life by it!

Toilet Time!

House tour is over! Now it's down to specifics. Show Mimi where her water bowl will always be. Let her investigate her crate. Then take her outside (still on leash) to the exact area where you want her to eliminate. Stand there until she does. (Patience! She's new at this.) Praise quietly *as* she goes, after which you can make the same kind of tour outside, with "leave it" warnings about flower or vegetable beds, bushes, or plants.

If you live in a city, by law (and responsible dog ownership) you must curb Mimi. Go to the quietest no-parking spot you can find. If you remain on the sidewalk, she will naturally want to join you, so stand down in the street with her. It will take time, plus your casual, confident attitude, to get her used to the noise, the confusion, and the speed and size of trucks and taxis.

No outside walking tour at this time. Wait until her immunizations are complete, by which time she will also be more accepting of city life. For now, it's only a bathroom break.

Note: If the original trip home from where you picked up Mimi took more than an hour, reverse the two "tours" to let the pup eliminate first. (For a complete housetraining program, see chapter 7.)

Back in the house, confine the puppy to the room you have puppy-proofed so she can investigate her new quarters. Encourage the cooperation of young children to "watch the puppy," but don't rely on them completely. Older kids, too, have good intentions, and the first week they may be just about perfect, but they have other things to do such as swim team or soccer practice, overdue homework, or a television program.

Confinement Indoors

By keeping the puppy in one safe room in your house, you are doing more than just keeping her safe. Mimi is learning to respect the limits you set. She is learning that you come and go and she doesn't have to panic when she hears you pick up the car keys. She is taking in all she needs to know about her new home and doing it all from a safe vantage point—safe from her viewpoint and yours.

A puppy learns more quickly from hearing "good dog!" than "bad dog!" For example, let's say while you were out she entertained herself by destroying your best running shoes. You come home, see the mess, and explode with *"Oh no! Bad dog! Why did you do that?"* and on and on. She has learned only that you are irrational and are not to be trusted. She was happily greeting you, and you went nuts! After all, she only chewed your shoes *because they were there!*

These Maltese are safe and out of trouble in their ex-pen.

A puppy given free run of the house is unable to put two and two together. She can't understand that when you corrected her for chewing the hall rug, you also meant the bedroom rug—and the bathmat, the bedspread, the sofa cushions, the telephone book, and everything else in the inventory of things *you* happen to value. Just think of all the punishments your puppy avoids when she is confined in a safe place. As far as the pup is concerned, "free run of the house" only means she is "free" to get into trouble and "free" to have people mad at her. And that is precisely what breaks down the very thing you need to establish— trust. Got it? Confinement equals "good dog."

The place where you choose to confine your pup when you can't be on puppy patrol may be your kitchen (with pet gates in doorways) or an exercise pen set up in any room that has destruction-free flooring. For short-term confinement, use the puppy's crate. A radio left on a "lite" or classical music station helps prevent separation anxiety when you're out of the room or the house. Dogs have exceptional hearing, so keep the volume low. The music and occasional voices relax the puppy, and the pup who is relaxed doesn't resort to excessive barking.

Confinement Outdoors

Two things keep a dog safe outdoors: one is a leash, the other is a fence. As Mimi grows up, you may want her to be outdoors part of the day. If you own your own property, you have a wide choice of fencing. When considering which kind, remember that dogs dig, climb, chew, and bark. (They also play, wag their tails, and let us know we're the best, which are the other reasons to invest in a safe fence!)

If there is something enticing, such as kids playing ball or a cat on the other side of the fence, that is reason enough for a dog to try to dig under or jump over the barrier. (Or just stand there and bark.) And if there is no such enticement, some dogs will make up their own reasons and dig anyway. (Siberian Huskies rate high on the "digger" chart.)

For the non-diggers (there are some), consistent training and the use of a pet repellent spray is enough. For the rest, or if you have no desire to find out the hard way, you'll need a fence installed with a twelve-inch wire extension below ground level and/or a trench of crushed stone. A sandbox or digging pit tucked in a corner of the yard might be the answer for a dedicated digger (it's called "directional digging"), or it might only encourage the dog to think all the world's a sandbox!

Solid wood fencing, such as stockade, offers some degree of noise deflection if your neighbors object to barking. It also provides a visual barricade to deter Mimi from barking at the sight of people, cats, or cars passing by.

This French Bulldog puppy will get into plenty of trouble in the yard, if you give her the chance.

If you opt for the newer electronic (sometimes called invisible) fencing, which gives the dog a shock from an electronic collar whenever she passes an invisible boundary, be aware that not all dogs can tolerate the stimulus and not all dogs can be taught to respect it. Terriers top the list of escapees because they have been bred specifically to withstand pain as well as to chase prey. They'll go after a squirrel, chipmunk, or the neighbor's cat without any concern about being zapped, prodded, or buzzed. Then, of course, they may not want to face being zapped on their return, when their adrenaline level is not as high—a perfect reason never to come home. Consider also the extent of power outages in your area.

Undesirable behavioral problems can result from this kind of fencing, as well. Some dogs become aggressive when confronted with pain. Others develop agoraphobia, or an intense fear of going outside. Animal behaviorists are seeing an increase in aggressive behavior toward both dogs and people in electronically controlled dogs.

The danger to all dogs is that this unseen fencing does not protect your property, including your dog, from roaming dogs or prevent any person (including dognappers) from coming onto your property. So your dog can easily be attacked or stolen. Likewise, you will be held liable if your neighbor's child or cat wanders onto your property and is attacked by your dog.

Perhaps fencing is not an option because you rent your home. A free-standing dog run is the answer for those dark and stormy nights (and equally dark early mornings) when Mimi has to go out but you'd rather stay inside, thank you! A free-standing dog run can be taken apart and go in the moving van when you move. It can also be moved from a shady spot in summer to a spot right by the back door in winter.

Wire tops are available to keep Super Dog from climbing out, as are awning-type tops to keep out rain, sun, and snow. A run can be set up on grass, concrete, or a bed of crushed stone. Drawbacks? Only one: It does not provide real physical exercise. Mimi will still need to be played with and walked after a pit-stop.

Leaving Your Dog Outdoors

Some breeds in some parts of the country will be kept outside all day while their owners are at work. There's no problem with this so long as the dog is *never* left tied up, which is cruel, unsafe, and causes undue stress. A secure dog run with an all-weather dog house, an adequate fresh water supply, and an appropriate variety of toys is part of the answer. The other part is for the first person home to bring Mimi indoors to be fed and be with the family. Dogs are social animals. They need to be with people and to take an active part in the "family pack."

Introducing the Crate

We're going to get a little bit ahead in housetraining here to make sure you understand how to introduce your puppy to the joys of a crate. Puppies are programmed by Mother Nature to keep their den clean, so all you have to do is to provide the "den" (crate) and stick to a schedule that allows your puppy to maintain that goal of cleanliness. Mimi may already have learned all about a crate and needs nothing more than to know where you keep it. Lucky you! For the rest of you new puppy owners, here's the procedure.

Don't worry if the puppy is more cautious than curious at first. She's being sensible about something that might be dangerous! *Do not* push, shove, or in any way try to force her into the crate. The situation calls for the art of gentle persuasion. Sweet-talk the puppy into overcoming any doubts by getting her interested in a toy and then tossing it into the crate. Or let her see and sniff a small treat in your hand *as* your hand goes into the crate. (Where a yummy treat goes, a pup is sure to follow.) As one paw steps inside, say "good dog—good *crate!*"

Slowly but Surely

Leave the door open for now, and if she does an instant turnaround (or backs out unceremoniously), that's normal. Make no comment, because Mimi is never praised for coming *out* of the crate, only for going in. Repeat this little scenario until the pup trots right in by herself. *Every* time you catch her about to step into the crate, be ready to say "good dog—good crate." Even if she's just looking for crumbs, it means she has accepted the idea that the crate is her own place. That's your goal.

Now begin to lure the puppy into the crate with a toy or a treat and close the door. Say "good dog" or "good crate" and then ignore her completely. Now is a good time to peel potatoes, read junk mail, or just pretend you're busy.

If Mimi reacts by whining or howling like a banshee, give the top of the crate a sharp tap *as* you say

Your dog's crate should be her safe haven.

Begin as you mean to continue. If you laugh at your puppy's misbehavior now, she will not understand when she is punished for it later.

"No! Quiet!" Then go back to the potatoes. If you keep glancing toward the crate, she will continue to fuss. That's a given. (You are catching on to the *"as"* timing, aren't you?)

Open the door to let Mimi out only when she is quiet—or even asleep. Gradually increase the length of time she stays in the crate with the door closed, until you reach half an hour or more. As the time increases, begin going in and out of the room, varying the amount of time you are in or out.

The exception to this crate-training process is overnight stays. From the first night, take the puppy out last thing before your bedtime, make sure she does her business, then put her in the crate (in your bedroom, if you wish) by tempting her with a small biscuit, and close the crate door. No conversation. She'll settle down if you ignore her. It's been a very busy day.

First thing in the morning—at the very first sound from Mimi—pick up the leash and Mimi, carry her to her potty area (or lead her, if she's too big to carry), and wait. It shouldn't take long this time. Then into her confined area.

Preventing Trouble

Prevention is the easiest, quickest, and surest way to discipline (that is, teach) your puppy. Invariably, the mischief (or, if left for more than a few minutes, full-blown destruction) your puppy got into will be discovered by you long *after* the fact. The pup who managed to chew through the leg of the coffee table obviously had not been watched for some time.

When you finally spot the damage, you do the normal thing: blow up! Just please don't blow up at your puppy. Shout "no!" only if Mimi is still hard at work. Whether caught in the act or not, give her a time out in her crate. During this time out, you can repeat ten times: *"I could have prevented that."*

You can't undo the damage, but you don't have to let it happen again. Be fair to yourself and to your puppy, who doesn't know antique cherry in the dining room from a fallen branch under a tree. Wood is wood.

Here are the rules for Puppy Punishment Prevention:

When Mimi is free with you in the house, *watch!*

When you can't watch, *crate.*

When you can't watch or crate (longer periods of time), *confine.*

No one is perfect. No puppy is perfect. There will be mishaps, but follow the rules and there won't be total disasters.

Part II
Your Growing Puppy

Chapter 5

Food, Exercise, and Care

There is not much your puppy wants more than his food—apart from you, that is! Since you are The Source of food, you score twice. You need to know how a puppy views food, because fussy or problem eaters are generally made, not born. Rapidly growing puppies have an intense desire as well as an obvious need to be fed—a puppy has to eat in order to grow. But the desire means food is a surefire way to get the puppy's attention, and that's where your teaching comes in.

Correctly used, food is a ready-made teaching tool. You can use it to teach a lot more than table manners. Feeding your puppy goes well beyond putting a bowl of dog food on the floor. Always ask for something in return—a sit, a paw, say "please," or whatever—but let the puppy know food comes with a price. If you fall for all the puppy's cute, darling, and adorable ways to beg for food, you will have a nuisance beggar for years to come.

Fresh, clean water is every bit as important as food, and should be available at all times.

Where and When to Feed

Dogs like to know exactly where and when meals will be served day after day. Pick a place to feed your puppy that is not a high-traffic area of the kitchen, then stick to that spot. The water bowl stays there. The food dish is put down and removed (empty or not) after fifteen to twenty minutes. For the first few days, stick with whatever feeding schedule your puppy has been on, so you don't upset his internal clock.

Some kennels and breeders use what is called the self-feeding method, which means a large amount of food is put out and the pup eats at will all day long. This method is *not* recommended, for several reasons. The first is that puppies tend to overeat. Pups of large breeds allowed to eat at will tend to grow too quickly and run the risk of skeletal problems. Smaller breeds risk becoming obese.

Apart from those health-related reasons, a puppy left alone all day with access to food tends to overeat out of sheer boredom. And a puppy who is allowed to eat all day long also needs to eliminate all day long, making housetraining difficult, to say the least.

On top of all that, you lose your role as provider, the offer of food ceases to be an exciting event, and food rewards lose their effectiveness as teaching tools. So, if your pup came home on a self-feeding schedule, take the next two or three days to put him on a more normal three-or-four-meals-a-day routine.

As for how many meals to give, from 8 to 12 weeks of age, feed the puppy four times a day. Avoid feeding him late at night by offering meals at 7 a.m., 11 a.m. (or noon), 3 p.m., and

This Bearded Collie needs clean water available right up until bedtime.

6 p.m. At about 12 weeks old, eliminate the late afternoon meal. Small to medium breeds should be fed three times a day until they are about 6 months of age, when you can cut back to feeding twice a day. Usually, a puppy will begin to leave some or most of the midday meal as an indication that it is no longer needed. Large breeds can remain on three meals a day until they are 12 or even 18 months, due to the danger of bloat from eating too much food at one time.

Fresh, clean water must be available until bedtime. That is just as important as food.

What to Feed

When you are feeding a rapidly growing puppy, the aim is not so much to satisfy his appetite, but to have him become as healthy an adult dog as possible. Your puppy should be eating a premium, high-quality growth or puppy food. The extra you pay for a premium puppy food could end up saving you large sums of money later in health care costs.

When the pup has reached 90 percent of his full height (between 9 to 12 months of age), it's time to switch to a maintenance diet that provides fewer calories. Large breeds such as German Shepherd Dogs, Golden Retrievers, and Labrador Retrievers can be switched over to a maintenance diet sooner to slow down their rate of growth, since they take longer to mature (12 to 24 months).

Which Food Is Best?

Keep your puppy on the same food he has been eating at the breeder's home, *unless* it is not a premium food especially formulated for puppies; or if your vet advises a different food; or if your puppy is not doing well on his food (check with the vet first). Then, and only then, is a change in order.

Your puppy's veterinarian will recommend a quality puppy food if you are confused by the array on the store shelves. Make the switch gradually to avoid stress or stomach upsets, and do it by *substituting* some of the new food for the old food—not by adding more food! Replace a small amount of the original food with the new. Increase the amount of new food each day as you decrease the old, until the change is complete. The whole process should take about a week.

Most breeders and canine nutritionists today agree that what's best for the dog—and what the dog likes best—is a combination of one-quarter canned dog food or meat mixed with three-quarters kibble (that is, dry) dog food. The meat or canned food is good for him and adds the taste and scent dogs enjoy, which encourages sluggish eaters. The majority of healthy puppies, however, tend to "inhale" their food, and the kibble slows them down, gives them chewing exercise, and also helps reduce tartar accumulation on the molars (the crushing teeth). For an 8- to 12-week-old puppy of a small breed, you could soak the kibble in a little warm water to soften it for tiny teeth, changing to dry as permanent teeth erupt. (Small-breed dogs will need small kibble bits all their lives, so make sure you choose a dry food made especially for small dogs or one with small pieces.)

Don't be tempted to add any vitamins or mineral supplements. Puppy or growth foods contain all the vitamins and minerals required by growing pups of all breeds or sizes. Adding more will upset the balance and cause dietary problems. For example, the correct proportion of calcium and phosphorus necessary for good bone growth is already in a quality growth food. Instead of helping your dog by supplementing, you could be doing irreparable harm.

Digestibility is important and something you can easily check. If as much is coming out of the dog as is going in, he is not absorbing enough nourishment.

All canned dog food, due to its high moisture content, can go bad quickly, so refrigerate leftovers. For a young puppy, warm it up slightly—at least to room temperature—before serving. The canned food labeled *meat with gravy* means

Reading Dog Food Labels

Dog food labels are not always easy to read, but if you know what to look for they can tell you a lot about what your puppy is eating.

- The label should have a statement saying the dog food meets or exceeds the American Association of Feed Control Officials (AAFCO) nutritional guidelines. If the dog food doesn't meet AAFCO guidelines, it can't be considered complete and balanced, and can cause nutritional deficiencies.
- The guaranteed analysis lists the minimum percentages of crude protein and crude fat and the maximum percentages of crude fiber and water. AAFCO requires a minimum of 18 percent crude protein for adult dogs and 22 percent crude protein for puppies on a dry matter basis (that means with the water removed; canned foods should have more protein because they have more water). Dog food must also have a minimum of 5 percent crude fat for adults and 8 percent crude fat for puppies.
- The ingredients list the most common item in the food first, and so on until you get to the least common item, which is listed last.
- Look for a dog food that lists an animal protein source first, such as chicken or poultry meal, beef or beef byproducts, and that has other protein sources listed among the top five ingredients. That's because a food that lists chicken, wheat, wheat gluten, corn, and wheat fiber as the first five ingredients has more chicken than wheat, but may not have more chicken than all the grain products put together.
- Other ingredients may include a carbohydrate source, fat, vitamins and minerals, preservatives, fiber, and sometimes other additives purported to be healthy.
- Some grocery store brands may add artificial colors, sugar, and fillers—all of which should be avoided.

you are paying for a large portion (about 80 percent) of moisture that contains little or no nutritional value. The canned chopped meat, or meat and rice formulated for puppies, is a better choice. The shelves are loaded with choices, but in the beginning, stick with one brand and one variety. That way you will know if the pup is vomiting because his stomach can't handle a certain food or due to something more serious. Save a gourmet menu for the adult dog.

The breeder of these Shetland Sheepdog pups is starting them off right with a high-quality diet.

There is another category of foods called semi-moist, made to look like the real thing—hamburger, ground chicken, or steak. They are handy for camping trips with an adult dog, but are not recommended for regular meals or for puppies, since they are high in sugar and can cause tartar build-up.

Treats

Treats are just like love: They are just as pleasurable to give as they are to receive. Just be sure you (and everyone else in the household) realize that treats are food. They should be doled out in tiny portions. If you reward your puppy with a treat and he lies down to chew it, it is too large. Consider it part of his dinner and reduce his evening meal accordingly. A true treat is a reward that's small enough to be swallowed after one crunch. It's just a taste.

The "goodnight, good dog" biscuit (more about that later) is a case in point. It is part of the pup's daily quota of food. When puppy grows up, you may decide to replace breakfast with a dog biscuit—an excellent solution for the overweight or under-exercised dog.

Bones

Just say no to bones. If you insist your dog needs a bone, buy a large sterilized bone at the pet supply store. Bones were given to dogs in the past because they satisfied the dog's need to chew and gnaw, and a bone from the butcher (or the dinner table) was all there was to give them. This was also before people worried

Pet Food vs. People Food

Many of the foods we eat are excellent sources of nutrients—after all, we do just fine on them. But dogs, just like us, need the right combination of meat and other ingredients for a complete and balanced diet, and a bowl of meat doesn't provide that. In the wild, dogs eat the fur, skin, bones, and guts of their prey, and even the contents of the stomach.

This doesn't mean your dog can't eat what you eat. A little meat, dairy, bread, some fruits, or vegetables as a treat are great. Fresh foods have natural enzymes that processed foods don't have. Just remember, we're talking about the same food you eat, not the gristly, greasy leftovers you would normally toss in the trash. Stay away from sugar, too, and remember that chocolate is toxic to dogs.

If you want to share your food with your dog, be sure the total amount you give him each day doesn't make up more than 15 percent of his diet, and that the rest of what you feed him is a top-quality complete and balanced dog food. (More people food could upset the balance of nutrients in the commercial food.)

Can your dog eat an entirely homemade diet? Certainly, if you are willing to work at it. Any homemade diet will have to be carefully balanced, with all the right nutrients in just the right amounts. It requires a lot of research to make a proper homemade diet, but it can be done. It's best to work with a veterinary nutritionist.

about the dangers of splintered bones getting stuck in the throat or intestinal tract, costing hundreds of dollars to remove. And long before anyone even thought about making toys especially for pets!

How Much to Feed

The feeding instructions on bags and cans of commercial dog foods are often too generous. Be guided by the fact that a young puppy will consume what his stomach can comfortably hold in about fifteen to twenty minutes, after which you should remove the dish. Do not leave it longer than that. This is The Source (you) at work, establishing good eating habits!

A good guide, however, is your puppy's appearance. His coat should be glossy, his eyes bright and clear, his teeth coming in straight and free of tartar. You should be able to feel but not see his ribs. A puppy who is too round and roly-poly is unhealthy. The puppy could have internal parasites or just be eating too many calories.

Most puppies, however, are convinced they are starving. Those pathetic whines and soulful eyes pleading for seconds (or dessert) could be masking a full stomach! Make sure you are not being conned. Obesity is the number one nutritional disorder in dogs of all ages. A puppy does not need diet food, but he does need diet management. Be sure the kids understand that puppies do not get pieces of jelly doughnuts, hamburger rolls, french fries, or other goodies under the table. Speaking of kids and goodies, remind everyone that chocolate is poisonous to dogs.

Puppies need more protein and fat in their diet than adult dogs do, so keep your puppy on a puppy or growth food until he is 1 year old.

What If the Puppy Doesn't Like the Food?

A puppy who doesn't eat *any food at all* for twenty-four hours should be taken to the veterinarian. Other than that, perhaps you are seeing a problem that doesn't exist. No healthy puppy who is offered food three or four times a day (and has it removed after fifteen minutes) ever starved. Dogs are manipulative, but not stupid! Conversely, a dog who eats well but appears to be genuinely hungry all day between meals should be checked by your veterinarian.

Dog Food Do's and Don'ts

Do keep small children away from the puppy while he's eating. A puppy is in the process of being taught that he does not have to guard his food. The dog regards little kids as a real threat because they are closer to the level of his dish! In addition, puppies often consider young children as littermates and therefore competitors, especially for food. So play it safe. A puppy (or an adult dog) may accept the child squatting down to watch him eat today, only to feel threatened and retaliate tomorrow.

Children are bitten because they do not understand the importance of food to an animal, and because the kids have not been taught that a danger exists. An older child of 7 or 8 will want to feed the puppy himself, but he still needs to be taught exactly how to do it, and that includes keeping a hands-off safe distance once the dog is eating.

From the beginning, show your pup that you are The Source of food and you are not to be messed with! Get him to watch you take a few kibbles out of his dish before putting it on the floor. Then let him eat them, as he would a treat, out of your hand—gently. If he nips or snatches, close your hand and stand up. Use the word "gentle" as he's licking your fingers. Then tell him "good dog" when he *is* gentle.

When he has learned to sit on command, he can do that before you put the dish down. Keeping your hand beside the dish for a moment establishes trust. If there's one growl or snarl, the dish is removed and Rufus is asked to sit again. Release him, wait a few minutes, and repeat the whole process. He's a smart puppy. He'll quickly catch on to your lesson in table manners!

In everything you do with and for your puppy, remember that you are teaching him. You are teaching him what you want him to do, how to do it, and that he can trust the people in his new family. Food is a major lesson in trust. A dog can't fix his own meals so he must trust you to do it, which is why consistency is so important. Same times, same place, same food.

Exercise

Right after food in importance to your puppy's growth (and pleasure) is exercise. Puppy workouts take many forms, some solo, some with members of his new family. Play, eat, and sleep are what puppies do best. (Okay, add piddle and poop.) Puppies can play alone, but the games they shared with their littermates were more fun, and now the members of his new family take on the role of playmates.

Jogging and running are *not* the right kind of exercise for a puppy, not even a big puppy. In fact, the larger the dog will be as an adult, the more you need to limit his hard physical exercise (including jogging, running, and jumping) until maturity. Have your veterinarian check the dog for soundness (heart, hips, etc.) at 12 to 18 months. Dogs will *always* try to keep up with you, to do whatever you ask them to do, so it is up to you to set the limits. Leaping over hurdles, two-mile trots, and flying Frisbee catches are for full-grown, physically sound adult dogs, not puppies. They can damage soft, growing bones.

Puppies should get most of their exercise from energetic play with four feet on the ground. Chase is a favorite because it is instinctive, so whether the "prey" is a large, indestructible ball for a Rottweiler puppy or a small squeaky toy rolled on the floor for a Yorkshire Terrier, the game is the same.

Your dog will want to go everywhere with you. Make sure your activities are appropriate for small puppies.

Roughhousing

While he was with his littermates, your puppy learned to roughhouse. It's still a great game, but don't let it go too far! You and your puppy should both avoid getting too physical with each other.

All physical interaction between you and your puppy should be at the pup's level of strength, ability, and understanding. A young puppy is just learning to trust, and if he is unintentionally hurt, will probably come back at you with teeth—which is just what he would do to a littermate. Don't punish. Apologize however you like, offer a quick tummy-rub to show there's no hard feelings, and get on with less strenuous play.

Overstimulation is stressful and can lead to aggressive behavior. Know when to quit—*before* play becomes frantic, *before* the pup is exhausted, and *before* there's more biting than mouthing.

If the puppy's activities have gone too far, stand up, fold your arms, and turn away as you say very calmly and firmly "settle" (or "steady" or "chill out" or whatever you like as long as it is the same *every time*). For a large, out-of-control puppy, lead him quietly to his crate for a time out. Let him out after two or three minutes and only when he is quiet. After all that, he will probably need to urinate.

It's okay when they play for these Schipperke pups to roughhouse with one another, but they should be more under control when they play with people.

Walking the Dog

There are different kinds of walks. One is the bathroom break or "business trip," which really isn't a walk at all. The puppy is on a leash and is taken to the place where he's meant to relieve himself, and you just wait until he does.

Another kind of walk is the training variety. The puppy is on a leash and be-bopping all over the place while you try to get him to trot next to you. Eventually he does, and with lots of practice you'll both graduate to the next two kinds of walks.

> ### T I P
>
> **Summer and Winter Walks**
>
> All exercise should be curtailed in warm weather and even eliminated when it gets hot. Heat stroke is dangerous at best, fatal at worst. Prevention is the best cure.
>
> Cold weather poses its own threats. Short-coated breeds and very small dogs may really feel the cold, and probably need a sweater when they go out. Beware also of the salt (or chemical) and sand mix used to melt ice and snow. Wash all four paws and any wet fur when you get home from a winter walk.

The exercise walk is the one we see so often these days. The person is getting his muscle tone up and excess fat down, and it is a very intense, no-nonsense, nonstop regimen. Dogs go along because they don't have a choice. This walk is strictly for adult dogs. Puppies need not apply.

Then there is the dog's walk, the one where Rufus gets to sniff everything along the way, to stop to greet other dogs and people, perhaps while you stop to buy a newspaper or feed the ducks. It is pure pleasure, the stuff canine heaven must be made of, and what's more, it is also very good for you. It is a calming form of exercise and allows you to teach as you go. Rufus learns to greet other dogs nicely, not jump up when you greet friends, and to sit or stand quietly when he is patted and admired.

For now this walk comes under the heading of "socializing your puppy," but this is the truly companionable walk that begins in puppyhood and is never outgrown.

Grooming

Maybe you think you can skip this section because you have a smooth-coated puppy whom you've been told doesn't need to be groomed. Guess again! *All* dogs must be groomed.

Even dogs with short coats, like these Chihuahuas, need some grooming.

As a bonus, your puppy will learn that it's okay to have someone go over every inch of his body, and there will be no trauma or stress when he is being examined by the vet, worked on by a professional groomer, touched by a trainer, or perhaps eventually given the once-over by an obedience trial or dog show judge. Besides, dogs think they are *very special* when they've had grooming attention.

Don't back off if your puppy objects to any portion of the grooming or he'll object more strenuously the next time. Anything from excessive wriggling to a snap or growl is corrected with an *"aacht!"* and then grooming continues at a nearby spot. For example, if this happens when you're cleaning out an ear, correct and then gently massage just in back of the ear with your fingers. Next time, *begin* with the comforting massage before getting on with the cleaning.

The point of grooming a new puppy is to get him used to being handled, to enjoy the hands-on physical attention. The results—beautification and health—are secondary benefits. In the process of grooming, your hands may find a tick or a lump that wasn't there last time, and your eyes may see fleas, a runny nose, tartar on teeth, and other indications of your pup's health. It's not just grooming. What you're doing amounts to teaching, bonding, and preventive medicine!

Where to Groom

Begin grooming with the puppy off the ground. About waist-high is a comfortable height to work. If you try to groom a dog on the ground, he has the advantage—you're on *his* turf and he's faster on four feet than you are on two! Get him up off the floor and *you* will be in control. If you don't have a grooming table, use any sturdy table, workbench, or countertop. Add a mat (a car floor mat or a thin rubber doormat are both good choices) so the pup will feel secure and won't slip.

In a pet supply store you can get a grooming arm that clamps onto any tabletop and which, with a hanging loop that is rather ominously known as a noose, will help keep the dog in place. There is always the danger of a puppy (or an adult dog) stepping off the edge of the grooming table, so get in the habit of keeping one hand (and both eyes) on the pup at all times, especially if you use a grooming noose.

A very tiny puppy—especially one with a long coat—may be brushed the first time or two lying in your lap so the pup is comfortable while you practice using the brush and comb. Grooming dogs (even puppies) with long coats does take time, so these puppies have to be taught to lie quietly on both sides while you work. It may be a struggle at first, but soon the dog will use the time to catch a nap.

Keep these first grooming sessions short—*very* short. Ten minutes, max. Always stop when the puppy is behaving nicely. *Never* end a session because the puppy is whining, growling, barking, biting, or acting up. If you do, you will have taught him that he can decide when it's quitting time. Instead, just go right on grooming, but do something he really likes to settle him down, add a "good dog" when his behavior is acceptable again, and *then* quit.

> ### TIPS
>
> #### Grooming Tools
>
> Bristle brush
>
> Soft slicker brush
>
> Clippers
>
> Flea comb
>
> Grooming glove
>
> Mat rake
>
> Nail clippers
>
> Scissors
>
> Shampoo
>
> Conditioner
>
> Tooth-cleaning equipment
>
> Towel

Grooming Tools

You also need the right tools for the job. For a smooth-coated pup, you need a soft bristle brush and a grooming glove or a rubber curry brush to stimulate the skin to keep it healthy and to distribute the natural oils in the coat. A good comb for a shorthaired puppy is a double-toothed flea comb (one side has finer teeth than the other). It will pull out any foreign objects, such as ticks, fleas, seeds, and burrs.

For a puppy with a thick, long, or wire coat, you will need a metal comb and a brush made for your puppy's coat type. If you missed that information when you got your puppy, a groomer or the pet supply store staff will help you choose the right brush. Pet supply catalogs also list pages of these grooming tools, many of which are designed specifically for certain breeds. If you decide on a slicker (bent-wire) brush, get the soft type for a puppy. Use it gently and only through the hair, because the wire will scratch the skin if you get carried away.

There are several types of tools made to break up mats, as well as special shedding tools for both long- and shorthaired dogs. Something for everyone!

Brushing

Brushing stimulates natural oils in the skin and hair, prevents mats, and helps keep your dog clean. Regular weekly brushing is a must, and for some longhaired breeds (Yorkshire Terriers are just one example), a quick daily brush-out is even better. If your dog ever looks untidy, scruffy, or matted, brush him!

Brushing is done from the skin out to the ends of the hairs, gently, slowly, and methodically on longhaired dogs. One mistake most people make is to brush only the ends of the hair or the top surface, so mats form close to the skin and in no time the pretty puppy has to be shaved.

Regular brushing is a must to keep your dog's coat clean, neat, and tangle-free.

Mats begin with a few tangled hairs, and are found most often under the front legs (behind the elbows) and behind the ears. They hurt your pup, so you *must* deal with them promptly. Work them out slowly and gently, first pulling the hairs apart with your fingers (or using the end tooth of the metal comb to pick the hairs apart), combing and brushing them straight as you go. A fine mist of plain water will reduce static electricity. Mats do not go away. They just get rapidly worse! If they are getting even slightly ahead of you, phone the groomer.

Trimming Nails

Nails need to be trimmed regularly, but what that means varies from dog to dog because their nails grow at different rates. If your dog's innocent interactions with you are causing scratches, it's about a week past the time you should have trimmed his nails.

Nail trimmers are made for small dogs (or puppies) and for big dogs whose large nails require a strong tool to do the job. There are two basic types of nail trimmers: one works like a regular scissors, and the other slices the nail guillotine-fashion when the two spring-operated handles are squeezed.

Only the tip that grows out beyond the quick is cut. On white nails, the quick is easier to see than on black nails; it's the pink part that runs through the inside of the nail. If you cut into the quick, it will bleed profusely. Styptic powder stops the bleeding, but it stings and the puppy won't be thrilled to let you cut his nails the next time! A dab of cornstarch will do almost as well, and won't sting.

Some dogs have an extra toe called a dewclaw on the inside of the leg above the foot. The nails on dewclaws must be trimmed, too.

It's easier to trim your dog's nails if you place him on a raised surface, as with this Bernese Mountain Dog.

Your vet or groomer can show you how to cut nails, or, if you are really not keen to learn how, regular trips to the groomer's for nail trimming are in order. Overgrown nails can cause a variety of problems, from painful walking to deformities requiring surgery.

Puppies are wiggly, but their nails are thinner and easier to cut than those of an adult dog. Start now with a weekly schedule, and by the time your pup is fully grown you will both have conquered nail trimming.

Ear and Eye Care

Using a clean, damp cloth, wipe the inside flap of the puppy's ears once a week. The inside of the ear has a natural light coating of wax that should not be removed. If the ear is really dirty (a long walk on a dusty road might do it), dampen a piece of gauze or cotton in mineral oil and gently wipe out the dirt. Be careful not to push dirt further into the ear. If there is a foul odor or excessive wax, consult your veterinarian. *Never* go into the ear canal with anything—not even a cotton swab. Not ever!

Clean around the eyes using a cotton ball dampened in clean warm water—one for each eye. Gently wipe away any accumulation of debris, and take the opportunity to check for mucus discharge, healthy eyelids, and clear, healthy-looking eyes.

In addition to wiping the ears and eyes, breeds with wrinkly faces, like this Pug, need to have the folds of skin on their faces wiped clean every day.

Tending to Teeth

The first teeth, or puppy teeth, fall out and the permanent set will erupt starting at about 4 or 5 months of age, at which time gums may be tender. Before then, get your puppy accustomed to your fingers going into his mouth. Gently lift his lips, one side at a time, and rub gently along the gums with your finger wrapped in a piece of gauze dampened with water. When he accepts that much, add a little canine toothpaste to the gauze. *People toothpaste is harmful to dogs.* There are several canine toothpaste varieties on the market.

Teeth need to be brushed twice a week to maintain dental health (dental problems are very expensive to treat!). Brushing also enables you to keep tabs on how the permanent teeth are erupting and whether or not your veterinarian needs to be alerted to any abnormality.

On permanent teeth you can use a regular soft-bristle toothbrush, but there are also special ones for dogs, as well as pads and even a small brush that fits on your finger. Or you can just continue to use gauze.

Anal Sacs

There is an anal sac on either side of your dog's anus, at approximately five and seven o'clock. Some dogs secrete dark brown anal sac fluid, which has a horrendous odor. In some dogs the anal sacs get clogged, or impacted, which is as uncomfortable as it sounds. You'll know anal sacs are the culprits if the dog is frantically trying to bite his tail or lick the area while dragging his backside on the ground.

Your veterinarian will first want to be sure the sacs are not infected or impacted. If not, he will probably express them for you—it is not a job anyone volunteers for! And if it will need to be done again, you'll be shown how. The good news is that most dogs do not have this problem.

Using Shampoo/Bathing

You *may* shampoo a young puppy, but it's better not to unless there is a valid reason, such as something dangerous or really dirty on the coat. However, it is hard to resist giving a little white ball of fluff a beauty treatment. First, thoroughly brush out the dog's coat. Mats will be impossible to untangle later. Then put a cotton ball in each ear to keep the water out.

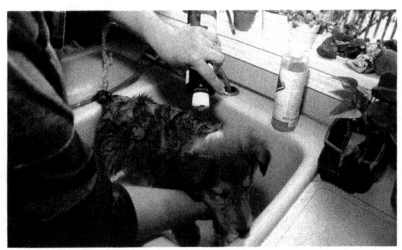

It's not hard to bathe a Collie puppy in the sink, but make sure he really needs a bath.

Work in a warm room. Use quite warm water (the pup's body temperature is higher than yours) and only use a shampoo made specifically for puppies. Put a towel in the sink or tub for safe footing, and use a spray attachment to help rinse out every bit of soap. You cannot rinse too much. Towel dry and/or blow dry with a hair dryer set on warm, *not* hot, and held at least eighteen inches or more away from the dog. Brush the coat carefully as it dries to avoid snarls and that enemy of long hair, mats.

Frequent shampooing destroys the natural oils in a dog's coat and can lead to dry skin problems. With good grooming habits, including rinsing off muddy feet, most dogs do not need a bath more than once a year. The exception is any of the long-coated breeds, especially those that require professional trimming.

Towel dry and snuggle your wet puppy. Be sure to keep him warm and away from drafts until he is completely dry.

Chapter 6

Keeping Your Puppy Healthy

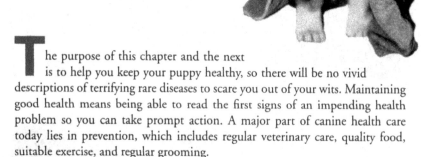

The purpose of this chapter and the next is to help you keep your puppy healthy, so there will be no vivid descriptions of terrifying rare diseases to scare you out of your wits. Maintaining good health means being able to read the first signs of an impending health problem so you can take prompt action. A major part of canine health care today lies in prevention, which includes regular veterinary care, quality food, suitable exercise, and regular grooming.

As luck would have it, problems are invariably first noted late at night, usually at bedtime. In fact, Murphy's Law might state that the more a situation is an emergency, the later at night it will occur. That's when you can check the information here, not—definitely *not*—to play doctor yourself, but to learn what might be wrong, what immediate action you can take, and what to relay to the vet when you do call. But an emergency, for example ingesting any sort of poison, calls for *immediate* action regardless of the time of day or night. Vomiting once, due to a honey bun you caught Mimi polishing off, can wait until morning.

Choosing a Veterinarian

Choosing a vet is difficult if you are new to pet ownership or if you've moved into a new area. One way to start is by asking friends and neighbors about local veterinarians, keeping in mind what kinds of pets they have and how their ideas of pet care coincide (or collide) with your own.

Veterinary practices are no longer limited to a waiting room, examination room, and surgery run by one person. Many today are in large complexes where all your pet's needs can be met under one roof—medical care, food, supplies, toys, grooming, boarding, training, and behavioral consultations. A veritable pet mall!

There are mobile vets who only make house calls and arrive with an equipped surgery right in the van. There are small animal hospitals with numerous doctors, and also the solitary vet who exchanges days off and holidays with a nearby doctor who has a similar practice. Then there are animal emergency centers manned around the clock, year-round, often with a small qualified permanent staff and area veterinarians taking turns on duty, some paid, some performing a community service. (You, of course, will be expected to pay.)

In other words, you have a lot to choose from—and having made a choice, you need never feel stuck with it. Feel free to call and ask if you may visit the office to meet the doctor. If the answer is "no," you might not feel welcome with your dog in tow, either.

You are the vital link between your dog and her doctor. The dog can't say what is bothering her or how she feels, so you must be able to communicate to the veterinarian how the dog's current actions (eating, eliminating, sleeping, and general behavior) differ from what is normal for your dog. If you are unable to have such an open conversation, feel cut off, or sense hostility or impatience, go elsewhere.

On the other side of the coin, *you must* listen to what the vet is saying, watch what he or she is showing you to do, and follow instructions to the letter.

You and your puppy should both feel comfortable with the veterinarian you choose.

When to Call the Veterinarian

Go to the vet right away or take your dog to an emergency veterinary clinic if:

- Your dog is choking.
- Your dog is having trouble breathing.
- Your dog has been injured and you cannot stop the bleeding within a few minutes.
- Your dog has been stung or bitten by an insect and the site is swelling.
- Your dog has been bitten by a snake.
- Your dog has been bitten by another animal (including a dog) and shows any swelling or bleeding.
- Your dog has touched, licked, or in any way been exposed to a poison.
- Your dog has been burned by either heat or caustic chemicals.
- Your dog has been hit by a car.
- Your dog has any obvious broken bones or cannot put any weight on one of her limbs.
- Your dog has a seizure.

Make an appointment to see the vet as soon as possible if:

- Your dog has been bitten by a cat, another dog, or a wild animal.
- Your dog has been injured and is still limping an hour later.

The perfect time to get to know a veterinarian and to establish the necessary confidence in the doctor, the staff, and the way the office is run is when you're taking care of those puppy shots. If you are not completely happy with your choice, as you become involved in the world of dogs (training classes, for example) you'll meet other dog owners with whom you can discuss other veterinarians.

Know Your Puppy

As you watch your puppy to fend off pranks, mischief, destruction, and disaster, you should also be observing what is normal for your pup—what she usually looks like (eyes, mouth, ears, body posture, energy level), how she behaves and reacts, how much she eats, drinks, and eliminates on a normal day. This casual observation will enable you to notice when something is wrong, when she's just

- Your dog has unexplained swelling or redness.
- Your dog's appetite changes.
- Your dog vomits repeatedly and can't seem to keep food down, or drools excessively while eating.
- You see any changes in your dog's urination or defecation (pain during elimination, change in regular habits, blood in urine or stool, diarrhea, foul-smelling stool).
- Your dog scoots her rear end on the floor.
- Your dog's energy level, attitude, or behavior changes for no apparent reason.
- Your dog has crusty or cloudy eyes, or excessive tearing or discharge.
- Your dog's nose is dry or chapped, hot, crusty, or runny.
- Your dog's ears smell foul, have a dark discharge, or seem excessively waxy.
- Your dog's gums are inflamed or bleeding, her teeth look brown, or her breath is foul.
- Your dog's skin is red, flaky, itchy, or inflamed, or she keeps chewing at certain spots.
- Your dog's coat is dull, dry, brittle, or bare in spots.
- Your dog's paws are red, swollen, tender, cracked, or the nails are split or too long.
- Your dog is panting excessively, wheezing, unable to catch her breath, breathing heavily, or sounds strange when she breathes.

not herself or has a runny nose, when she's limping slightly, not eating well, urinating more than normal, and so on.

Take the time, every day, to run your hands over your puppy. You can do this as a good morning cuddle, or while you're grooming her. But don't just pet and brush her; run your fingers through and under her coat so you can feel right down to the dog's skin. If she picks up a tick, you will feel it with your fingers. If she has a cut, a lump, a bruise, or a skin rash, you will feel it. If she's getting too chubby or skinny for her age and breed, you'll know.

By checking the dog this way every day, you will discover these things before they turn into bigger problems. When you start this routine in puppyhood, your dog will come to love it, and will be more accepting of being petted by other people—especially the veterinarian—as an adult.

Obviously, the best time for a thorough examination is after you have brushed your puppy, which may be only once a week. Start at her head and, using your fingertips to navigate through the fur, feel all over your puppy's head, including around her muzzle, eyes, ears, and neck. Take your time and be gentle; think of it as giving your puppy a massage.

Continue working your hands down your puppy's body, examining her shoulders, back, sides, legs, and tail. Run your hands down each leg, handling each toe on each paw, checking for burrs and foxtails, cuts and scratches. Check your puppy's nails. They need regular trimming, every week or two. A routine check will tell whether any nails are chipped or cracked and accustom the puppy to having her feet handled.

As your puppy's caretaker, you need to know what is normal for her. Changes in attitude or activity level can be a sign of a problem.

If you find any minor cuts and scrapes, you can wash them with soap and water and apply a mild antibiotic ointment. However, if a cut is gaping or looks red and inflamed, call your veterinarian. Check your puppy's tummy, too. Fleas like to hide in the groin area, in front of the tail, and behind elbows—don't miss those spots. Ticks latch on anywhere.

Once you've gone over her entire body this way, return to her head. It's time to check your puppy's mouth, looking for inflamed gums, foreign objects, and cracked or broken teeth. Become familiar with what the teeth look like, especially as the puppy teeth fall out and the permanent ones come in.

Next, clean only the parts inside of the ears that you can see (*never* go down into the ear canal). Gently wipe the inside of the ears with cotton balls (or a piece of gauze wrapped around your finger) lightly moistened with warm water or a commercial product made especially for cleaning canine ears. As you wipe out the ear, check for scratches or foreign objects and give the ear a sniff. If there is quite a bit of discharge and/or the ear has a sour smell, call your veterinarian; your puppy may have an ear infection.

Immunizations

Healthy puppies need to be immunized against several potentially lethal diseases so they can stay healthy. Breeders will generally have taken care of their puppies' first set of shots, sometimes even the second set, depending upon the age at the time of sale. From then on it's up to you to follow a schedule set by you and your veterinarian.

Immunizations provide protection against contagious diseases that can be (and usually are) fatal in young puppies, so the series is a very inexpensive form of health insurance. As a bonus, each time you take your puppy in for shots, the veterinarian will check the pup's general physical condition and growth, and answer your questions. Well worth the price of admission!

Always be extremely observant of your pup's reaction to all immunizations and medications. Report anything unusual to your vet. Basic annual routine check-ups by your veterinarian may, if you wish, include taking blood samples to evaluate the titers, or the level of immunization still present. In any event, your vet will remind you when to bring Mimi in for routine check-ups. They are an essential part of preventive care.

Your new puppy should have already had one set of puppy shots, but will need more.

Vaccines

What vaccines dogs need and how often they need them has been a subject of controversy for several years. Researchers, health care professionals, vaccine manufacturers, and dog owners do not always agree on which vaccines each dog needs or how often booster shots must be given.

In 2003, the American Animal Hospital Association released vaccination guidelines and recommendations that have helped dog owners and veterinarians sort through much of the controversy and conflicting information. The guidelines designate four vaccines as core, or essential, because of the serious nature of the diseases and their widespread distribution. These are canine distemper virus, canine parvovirus, canine adenovirus-2, and rabies. The general recommendations for their use (except rabies, for which you must follow local laws) are:

- Vaccinate puppies at 6–8 weeks, 9–11 weeks, and 12–14 weeks.
- Give a booster shot when the dog is 1 year old.
- Give a subsequent booster shot every three years, unless there are risk factors that make it necessary to vaccinate more or less often.

Spay/Neuter

Another important aspect of preventive care is spaying (for females) and neutering (for males). Myths abound about these procedures, but the facts are plain and simple: they are extremely beneficial to your pet's health. Either operation is performed when the pup is about 6 months of age, or just approaching sexual maturity, but discuss with your vet the best time for your puppy. It is a minor operation from which the pup recovers quickly. The major benefit is that you, as a responsible pet owner, will have eliminated any chance of adding to the overpopulation of unwanted puppies.

Noncore vaccines should only be considered for those dogs who risk exposure to a particular disease because of geographic area, lifestyle, frequency of travel, or other issues. They include vaccines against distemper-measles virus, canine parainfluenza virus, leptospirosis, Bordetella bronchiseptica, and Borrelia burgdorferi (Lyme disease).

Vaccines that are not generally recommended because the disease poses little risk to dogs or is easily treatable, or the vaccine has not been proven to be effective, are those against Giardia, canine coronavirus, and canine adenovirus-1.

Often, combination injections are given to puppies, with one shot containing several core and noncore vaccines. Your veterinarian may be reluctant to use separate shots that do not include the noncore vaccines, because they must be specially ordered. If you are concerned about these noncore vaccines, talk to your vet.

Spaying involves the removal of the uterus, fallopian tubes, and ovaries. It will *not* cause your adorable Mimi to become obese. That's a myth. To keep her weight under control, don't overfeed her and do provide her with sufficient exercise.

Neutering is the removal of both testicles in the male dog. It will *not* turn Rufus into a wimp, or change your dog's personality—except perhaps to calm aggressive outbursts when encountering other male dogs. He will still protect you and be as good a watchdog as ever. Neutering will *not* cause him to get fat. Overfeeding and underexercising, however, will.

Why Spay and Neuter?

Breeding dogs is a serious undertaking that should only be part of a well-planned breeding program. Why? Because dogs pass on their physical and behavioral problems to their offspring. Even healthy, well-behaved dogs can pass on problems in their genes.

Is your dog so sweet that you'd like to have a litter of puppies just like her? If you breed her to another dog, the pups will not have the same genetic heritage she has. Breeding her *parents* again will increase the odds of a similar pup, but even then, the puppies in the second litter could inherit different genes. In fact, *there is no way to breed a dog to be just like another dog.*

Meanwhile, thousands and thousands of dogs are killed in animal shelters every year simply because they have no homes. Casual breeding is a big contributor to this problem.

If you don't plan to breed your dog, is it still a good idea to spay her or neuter him? Yes!

When you spay your female:

- You avoid her heat cycles, during which she discharges blood and scent.
- It greatly reduces the risk of mammary cancer and eliminates the risk of pyometra (an often fatal infection of the uterus) and uterine cancer.
- It prevents unwanted pregnancies.
- It reduces dominance behaviors and aggression.

When you neuter your male:

- It curbs the desire to roam and to fight with other males.
- It greatly reduces the risk of prostate cancer and eliminates the risk of testicular cancer.
- It helps reduce leg lifting and mounting behavior.
- It reduces dominance behaviors and aggression.

There is no way to breed a dog who is exactly like any other dog. These Rhodesian Ridgeback littermates may look the same, but they do not have the same genes or the same personalities.

In fact, some of those myths came about because dog owners were told (and wanted desperately to believe) that behavior problems would change for the better or all disappear after neutering the dog. Sorry, folks! Only certain sex-related behaviors change. Changing undesirable behavior is up to you—with help from your obedience trainer or a canine behaviorist.

Giving Your Puppy Medicine

Some medicines are easy to administer, some are not. Some puppies will take pills or let you put ointment in their eyes easily, some will not. Ask your veterinarian for assistance if you have a problem following these helpful instructions.

To put eye ointment in the eye without poking the puppy with the tube, stand behind your puppy and cuddle her head up against your chest or legs. With one hand, gently pull the lower eyelid away from the eye just slightly. At the same time, squeeze some of the ointment into the lower eyelid. When the puppy blinks, the medication will be distributed over the eye.

There are different ways to give your puppy a pill. One easy way is to dip the pill in a jar of meat baby food and let your pup lick it off your hand. (Watch to be sure she doesn't spit out the pill.) Another very easy way is to wedge the pill in a piece of cheese or meat that is just large enough to enclose it. Give the pup one tiny piece of cheese or meat, then the one with the pill in it. One gulp and it's gone! With both these methods, check with your vet first to make sure the medication can be given with food.

Still another way to give a pup a pill is to gently pull your puppy's head up and back so her muzzle is pointing up. Open her mouth and quickly drop the pill on the back of her tongue. Close her mouth and massage her throat until she swallows. Before you let her go, open her mouth and check to see that the pill is gone.

To give liquid medication, measure the medicine in a needle-less syringe, put the tip inside the puppy's cheek from the corner of her mouth and, holding the puppy's mouth shut, squirt the medication in while you tilt her head slightly backward so the medicine runs right into the mouth. Squeeze the syringe slowly so the puppy is able to swallow the liquid without choking.

Applying a skin ointment is usually very easy—just part the hair so you're putting the ointment directly on the skin and rub it in according to directions. Keeping your puppy from licking the ointment off can be more difficult, and licking often makes matters worse. If your puppy has a bad skin condition or stitches that need to heal, your veterinarian will probably give you an Elizabethan collar for her. Named for the high collars that were in fashion during the reign of Queen Elizabeth I, this is a large plastic collar that extends to the tip of your puppy's nose. The collar is clumsy, and most puppies absolutely hate it, but it's an excellent way to give the wound a chance to heal.

Give your puppy all the medicine your vet prescribes, even if she seems to be getting better.

Whenever your veterinarian prescribes a treatment or medication, don't be afraid to ask questions. Ask what the drug is, what it does, and how long your puppy should take it. Ask if there are any side effects you should watch for. Make sure you understand what your puppy's problem is, what the course of treatment will do, and what you should (or should not) expect. Then, make sure you follow through on the course of treatment. If your veterinarian said to give the medication for ten days, give it for ten days. Don't stop at five days just because your puppy looks better. Again, if you have any problems or reservations, call your vet.

Internal Parasites

All the parasites listed below are treatable after diagnosis, usually examination of your puppy's stools. If you see anything moving in your puppy's stool, or you see small worms crawling near her anus or small bits of what look like dried rice deposited where she has been sitting, it's likely she has internal parasites. You may not see any signs at all, though, which is why regular stool checks are important.

Don't try to treat suspected worms yourself, because the "cure" is actually a poison to kill the worms. It could harm your puppy if it is incorrectly administered. In addition, not all over-the-counter wormers work for all types of worms. Your puppy needs a definitive diagnosis and a specific course of treatment. And for that, she needs to see your veterinarian.

All kinds of worms and parasites lurk in seemingly innocent gardens. Watch your pup for signs of problems and bring regular stool samples to your vet for a check.

Roundworm is a very common internal parasite in young puppies. Take a fresh stool sample on your first visit to the vet so it can be checked for worms. Roundworms are easy to treat, but can cause serious problems if left untreated.

Hookworm eggs burrow into the skin through a puppy's feet or are acquired by eating an infected animal's stools. In the body, hookworms migrate to the dog's small intestines, where they latch on and suck blood. When the worms detach and move, they leave open wounds behind, causing bloody diarrhea—the first sign of infection. People can get hookworm from infected soil, too.

Some heartworm preventives will also keep away other parasites. Ask your veterinarian what's best for your dog.

Whipworms feed on blood in the large intestine, and a heavy infestation leaves a puppy looking thin, usually with watery or bloody diarrhea. Whipworm eggs can live in soil for many years and can be acquired by eating new grass, digging up a bone, or licking the dirt.

Tapeworms also grow in the dog's intestines, where they absorb nutrients from the intestinal wall. They're acquired by swallowing fleas, the intermediary host. You can tell if your dog has tapeworm by noticing white rice-like segments in her feces. These are the segments of growing tapeworms.

Heartworm infestation is passed on to the dog by a bite from a mosquito, which is the intermediary host between infected animals. The worm itself grows in the chambers of the heart and is almost always fatal. The treatment involves the use of arsenic to kill the heartworm, itself a dangerous procedure. Heartworm preventives are available in the form of a pill that is given every day or every thirty days. These should only be used *after* your veterinarian has obtained a negative result from a blood test. When the medication is started and how long it is continued depends on the incidence of heartworm in your area. In most of the United States now it is administered year-round. The medication also controls hookworm, whipworm, and roundworm, making it another excellent investment in your pup's good health.

Fleas

Fleas are a prolific, common environmental enemy of people and animals. Despite the number of products on the market to rid the dog, the house, and the garden of this pest, the flea continues to thrive.

The first thing to do is accept the fact that if you discover one flea on your pet, your house probably contains thousands of fleas in various stages of growth. Treating the dog will make her more comfortable temporarily, and will inhibit the further growth of flea eggs or larvae on the dog or when they drop off onto your carpet. However, the very first thing to do is actually two things at the same time: clean your home and your dog.

Ticks

Ticks are rapidly catching up with fleas in many areas of the country as the most invasive insect, especially the tiny deer ticks (found on whitetail deer and white-footed mice) that are the carriers of Lyme disease, which infects dogs and humans.

The first sign of Lyme disease is a round red targetlike spot on the skin, which is easily seen on a person but not on a furry dog! The next symptoms are fever, lethargy, and a swollen joint with intense arthritic-like pain. Check with your veterinarian if any of these things are apparent, especially if they occur after you have removed a tick. Antibiotics are successful in treating Lyme disease.

Check your dog's body carefully for ticks after every outdoor romp. Ticks carry serious diseases that can be fatal for a puppy.

New Products in the Fight Against Fleas

At one time, battling fleas meant exposing your dog and yourself to toxic dips, sprays, powders, and collars. But today there are flea preventives that work very well and are safe for your dog, you, and the environment. The two most common types are insect growth regulators (IGRs), which stop the immature flea from developing or maturing, and adult flea killers. To deal with an active infestation, experts usually recommend a product that has both.

These next-generation flea fighters generally come in one of two forms:

- **Topical treatments or spot-ons.** These products are applied to the skin, usually between the shoulder blades. The product is absorbed through the skin into the dog's system. Among the most widely available spot-ons are Advantage (kills adult fleas and larvae), Revolution (kills adult fleas), Frontline Plus (kills adult fleas and larvae, plus an IGR), K-9 Advantix (kills adult fleas and larvae), and BioSpot (kills adult fleas and larvae, plus an IGR).
- **Systemic products.** This is a pill your dog swallows that transmits a chemical throughout the dog's bloodstream. When a flea bites the dog, it picks up this chemical, which then prevents the flea's eggs from developing. Among the most widely available systemic products are Program (kills larvae only, plus an IGR) and Capstar (kills adult fleas).

Make sure you read all the labels and apply the products exactly as recommended, and that you check to make sure they are safe for puppies.

How to Get Rid of a Tick

Although Frontline, K-9 Advantix, and BioSpot, the new generation of flea fighters, are partially effective in killing ticks once they are on your dog, they are not 100 percent effective and will not keep ticks from biting your dog in the first place. During tick season (which, depending on where you live, can be spring, summer, and/or fall), examine your dog every day for ticks. Pay particular attention to your dog's neck, behind the ears, the armpits, and the groin.

When you find a tick, use a pair of tweezers to grasp the tick as close as possible to the dog's skin and pull it out using firm, steady pressure. Check to make sure you get the whole tick (mouth parts left in your dog's skin can cause an infection), then dab the wound with a little hydrogen peroxide and some antibiotic ointment. Watch for signs of inflammation.

Ticks carry very serious diseases that are transmittable to humans, so dispose of the tick safely. *Never* crush it between your fingers. Don't flush it down the toilet either, because the tick will survive the trip and infect another animal. Instead, use the tweezers to place the tick in a tight-sealing jar or plastic dish with a little alcohol, put on the lid and dispose of the container in an outdoor garbage can. Wash the tweezers thoroughly with hot water and alcohol.

Dogs can now be vaccinated annually against Lyme disease. Ask your veterinarian if it's appropriate for your dog, and at what age your dog should begin receiving it.

The most common variety of tick is the brown dog tick. It is about the size of a match head, but grows to the size of a pebble when engorged with blood. Deer ticks are about the size of a sesame seed even when engorged, and are extremely difficult to detect on your dog. Look for ticks behind the ears (or on them), on the neck and tummy, behind the elbows, between the toes, and on the flanks.

Making Your Environment Flea Free

If there are fleas on your dog, there are fleas in your home, yard, and car, even if you can't see them. Take these steps to combat them.

In your home:

- Wash whatever is washable (the dog bed, sheets, blankets, pillow covers, slipcovers, curtains, etc.).
- Vacuum everything else in your home—furniture, floors, rugs, everything. Pay special attention to the folds and crevices in upholstery, cracks between floorboards, and the spaces between the floor and the baseboards. Flea larvae are sensitive to sunlight, so inside the house they prefer deep carpet, bedding, and cracks and crevices.
- When you're done, throw the vacuum cleaner bag away—in an outside garbage can.
- Use a nontoxic flea-killing powder, such as Flea Busters or Zodiac FleaTrol, to treat your carpets (but remember, it does not control fleas elsewhere in the house). The powder stays deep in the carpet and kills fleas (using a form of boric acid) for up to a year.
- If you have a particularly serious flea problem, consider using a fogger or long-lasting spray to kill any adult and larval fleas, or having a professional exterminator treat your home.

Mites and Mange

Ear mites are another kind of pesky external parasite. They are microscopic bugs that live in the ear canal, causing an infection or irritation common in puppies and young dogs. You'll suspect infection by the way the pup scratches her ears or violently shakes her head to relieve the intense itching.

Dogs' ears are extremely sensitive, so it's better not to go probing around in the ear canal beyond the normal, gentle cleaning of the outer ear area (the part you can easily see). Don't try to treat ear mites yourself, regardless of how many products you may find in the pet supply store. Let your veterinarian diagnose the problem and show you exactly how to treat it. Ear mites are persistent little bugs, and you'll have to keep up the treatment until they are well and truly gone.

In your car:

- Take out the floor mats and hose them down with a strong stream of water, then hang them up to dry in the sun.
- Wash any towels, blankets, or other bedding you regularly keep in the car.
- Thoroughly vacuum the entire interior of your car, paying special attention to the seams between the bottom and back of the seats.
- When you're done, throw the vacuum cleaner bag away—in an outside garbage can.

In your yard:

- Flea larvae prefer shaded areas that have plenty of organic material and moisture, so rake the yard thoroughly and bag all the debris in tightly sealed bags.
- Spray your yard with an insecticide that has residual activity for at least thirty days. Insecticides that use a form of boric acid are nontoxic. Some newer products contain an insect growth regulator (such as fenoxycarb) and need to be applied only once or twice a year.
- For an especially difficult flea problem, consider having an exterminator treat your yard.
- Keep your yard free of piles of leaves, weeds, and other organic debris. Be especially careful in shady, moist areas, such as under bushes.

Mange is also caused by mites, and comes in two types. Demodectic mange results in a loss of hair around the nose, mouth, and eyelids in puppies. It tends to improve on its own, but don't ignore it! When it does get worse, with patches appearing almost anywhere on the dog, the treatment is long and not always successful. To put your mind at ease, check with your vet at the first sign of mange.

Sarcoptic mange (also called scabies) may be seen as a red rash (mite bites) with crusts or scabs. It is intensely itchy and appears mostly on ear tips and elbows. These mites are not too fussy about where they land, and you'll know they've picked on you if you are feeling itchy around your waistline. Don't panic. With normal cleanliness, it disappears in about three weeks. But do consult your veterinarian for a dip that will eliminate the problem on the dog in four to six weeks.

Dogs can be plagued by a wide variety of itches, from fleas to skin allergies to mange. Take them all seriously and don't let them torment your pup.

Skin Ailments

Dogs' allergies are generally manifested as itchy skin, and are primarily caused by ingesting or inhaling such things as grasses, weeds, and pollen. They can also be caused by foods—reactions to wheat, soy, and beef are common. Contact allergies are less common but can be caused by something as innocuous as man-made fiber rugs or dog bedding. A change to pure cotton or wool is the simple solution. Mild skin irritations are often controlled by special shampoos.

Once the allergen has been detected, the "cure" may be simply to avoid the culprit, as, for example, in the case of a reaction to wheat or beef. More complex cases require veterinary testing and antigen shots over a long period of time. This is the same desensitizing treatment people receive and, like the human treatment, it can be costly and time-consuming.

Hot spots are intensely itchy spots on the skin that worsen as the dog licks or scratches them. The most common cause is a flea bite. If you catch it when the spot is small, clean it with an antibiotic spray and spread a taste deterrent such as Bitter Apple on the surrounding hair to keep the dog from irritating it. Work hard on getting rid of the fleas. If the area is large when you discover it, consult your veterinarian. It may be more than just a hot spot.

Ringworm is not a worm at all, but a fungus that grows under the skin in a circle, with loss of hair in the center. This is a highly contagious disease that can be transmitted both ways—from dogs to people or people to dogs. Caught early enough, you can treat it yourself with Tinactin (from the drugstore), but keep the kids away from the dog until the cure is complete.

First Aid and Emergencies

Your puppy cannot tell you when she is sick, but if you spend enough time with her and are observant of her behavior, you'll notice when she's feeling off. The following are examples of problems that require first aid.

Snow Nose

Snow nose has no known cause or cure, but it is only a cosmetic problem, not a matter of health. The condition refers to a normally dark-colored nose that gradually loses pigmentation, usually in the winter, and regains it come summertime. Some dogs just seem to outgrow it. Occasionally, as a dog matures, the snow nose becomes a permanent discoloration, anything from charcoal gray (or dusty rose in a nose that is normally a liver color) to white.

First aid is what you do to assist a dog in an emergency situation, *before you reach the vet's office.* Such assistance should be minimal, so as not to make matters worse, and it must be safe for the dog and for you. If possible, alert the veterinarian immediately.

The first rule of canine first aid is to remain completely calm and (outwardly at least!) in control of the situation. The second rule is to fight off the desire to pick up or lean over to comfort a hurt dog face to face, the way you would a child. When hurt and frightened, a dog's instinct for self-preservation takes over; he is likely to bite whatever comes near. That's where safety comes in.

Because hurt dogs bite, almost every injured dog should be muzzled. Before attempting to muzzle your dog, though, be certain he is breathing normally, since limited breathing could be made worse by keeping the dog's mouth closed. Don't have a muzzle handy? No problem. A neck-tie, pantyhose, two feet of rope, a scarf, or a dog leash will do nicely. Tie a loose knot in the middle and slip the loop of the knot over the middle of the dog's muzzle. Pull it firm and tie the two ends under the dog's chin, then in back of the dog's ears. (Make that last tie a bow so it will untie easily to pull forward and off the muzzle.)

How to Make a Canine First-Aid Kit

If your dog hurts herself, even a minor cut, it can be very upsetting for both of you. Having a first-aid kit handy will help you to help her, calmly and efficiently. What should be in your canine first-aid kit?

- Antibiotic ointment
- Antiseptic and antibacterial cleansing wipes
- Benadryl
- Cotton-tipped applicators
- Disposable razor
- Elastic wrap bandages
- Extra leash and collar
- First-aid tape of various widths
- Gauze bandage roll
- Gauze pads of different sizes, including eye pads
- Hydrogen peroxide
- Instant cold compress
- Kaopectate tablets or liquid
- Latex gloves
- Lubricating jelly
- Muzzle
- Nail clippers
- Pen, pencil, and paper for notes and directions
- Pepto-Bismol
- Round-ended scissors and pointy scissors
- Safety pins
- Snake-bite kit
- Sterile saline eyewash
- Thermometer (rectal)
- Tweezers

Dogs with short muzzles or no discernible bridge, such as Pugs, Pekingese, and Bulldogs, are not candidates for a makeshift muzzle. In fact, don't do anything that might interfere with their breathing. If you have assistance, a rolled-up blanket, towel, or a pillow can be held (gently, but firmly) around the dog's neck while treating the injury.

Your puppy will rely on you to be calm in an emergency.

Shock is the breakdown of the cardiovascular system, and immediate veterinary care is essential. Many things, such as dehydration or poisoning, may cause a dog to go into shock, but being hit by a car is the major cause of shock.

Electrical shock is the fate of a puppy left to chew on an electric cord his owner forgot to put up out of reach. The result is a nasty burn to the mouth that, while painful, will heal in time. More serious are lightning strikes or touching downed wires. In either case the dog (if not killed) is burned and also suffers circulatory collapse and pulmonary edema (the lungs fill with fluid). If the dog is unconscious and not breathing, give artificial respiration (see page 92). No matter what the dog's condition, get him to a veterinarian immediately.

Car accidents still account for most canine deaths, which is a sad commentary on the way we keep our dogs. All it takes to keep your dog safe is a leash or a fence and basic obedience training. No matter how slight the injury may seem, any dog hit by a car requires immediate emergency treatment by a veterinarian. There may be internal injuries or bleeding, broken bones, concussion, and shock.

Check for external bleeding and stop it by applying a pressure bandage or just holding a bandage or clean padded cloth over the wound. Spurting blood

The Emergency Hospital

Because all kinds of emergencies can happen to your puppy when your regular veterinary clinic is closed, it's important to have an emergency number to call. Ask your veterinarian for this number on your first visit, and keep it by the phone. You won't want to be scrambling for it when a real emergency strikes. And you won't want to be struggling with directions in the middle of the night if you've never been to the emergency clinic before. It's a good idea to do a practice run to the clinic when it's not an emergency. You'll need all the calm you can muster in a real emergency, and knowing how long it will take to get to the clinic is important.

indicates a severed artery, which can be controlled by applying pressure on the artery.

Moving an injured dog other than a very small one requires two people and a board, bench, sled, or any improvised stretcher, or a blanket held taut. Do not muzzle a dog in shock, but keep the dog quiet and transfer him immediately to the veterinarian.

When a board is the means of transportation, be sure the dog is securely tied to it with strips of sheeting or rope. An injured animal panics easily and could do himself further damage in struggling to escape.

Burns are caused by many things, such as touching a hot surface, fire, and even sunburn. Severe burns of any kind can progress to shock, and the prognosis then is poor. Small, superficial burns can be treated by soaking the area with cold water or ice packs for fifteen to twenty minutes to relieve the pain. Then trim the surrounding hair, wash with surgical soap, and gently blot dry. Apply antibiotic ointment. If the area needs protection (for example, when the dog lies down or walks), wrap it loosely with gauze.

Bleeding is one of the primary reasons for first aid. Minor bleeding can be stopped by cleaning the area with an antiseptic, applying a gauze pad, then bandaging with even pressure using gauze or any clean material available. Watch for signs of swelling or discoloration below the bandage, which indicates a loss of circulation—in which case loosen or remove the bandage immediately.

Minor play scuffles between dogs rarely result in broken skin, but be sure to check and to wash and treat all wounds, no matter how small.

Arterial bleeding comes in bright red spurts and requires a thick pressure pad (as above), plus additional pressure applied by hand. A tourniquet can be applied to the tail or leg above the wound, between the wound and the heart, but it must be loosened every twenty-five to thirty minutes and is best left to a professional.

Broken bones may be made worse by handling. In puppies the most common break is a greenstick fracture, in which the bones bend and crack or splinter. A compound fracture (where the skin is pierced by the broken bone) should first be covered with a clean cloth. Immobilize the area and transport the dog (preferably on a rigid surface) to a veterinarian as carefully and as quickly as possible.

Cuts and abrasions should be washed with warm soap and water, then rinsed with cold water to help stop bleeding. Apply an antiseptic spray or ointment.

Dog fights are very dangerous for dogs and people. If two dogs cannot be pulled apart by their leashes, separating them is best left to a pair of strong men, who will probably be bitten in the process no matter what means of separation they try. A hard stream of cold water may work sometimes, but not often enough to recommend it. Throwing a coat or blanket over the two dogs' heads will often cause one of the dogs to let go for an instant—but in that instant someone has to be ready to pull them apart by their tails or hindquarters.

A shrill personal alarm may work. Mace or mace-type spray may also work. Avoid inflicting pain on either dog, because it will only increase the dog's aggression. Avoid giving the appearance of siding with either dog. Clean all bite wounds thoroughly, especially small puncture wounds, and get the dog(s) to the veterinarian at once.

Dogs do not know how to swim naturally, and too often they get into the water, manage to swim a short distance, and then are unable to get out. **Drowning** is a very real possibility. This is especially true in swimming pools or when a dog breaks through ice on a pond or lake. Treatment is the same as for people. Get the dog onto land immediately, clean out his mouth, give artificial respiration (see page 92) or even oxygen, if available. Be prepared to treat for shock.

Hypothermia occurs when a dog is exposed to extreme cold. For some dogs, just getting wet and moderately cold will cause the body temperature to drop dangerously. Bring the dog into a warm room. Wrap her in blankets, rub her with towels, and place hot water bottles (containing warm water) under her armpits, chest, and stomach. When her rectal temperature reaches 100 degrees, feed her honey or sugar and water.

Heat stroke (hyperthermia) requires immediate action. Most dogs suffering from heatstroke were left in cars. Even with the windows partially open and the car parked in the shade, on a moderately warm day it only takes minutes for the inside of a car to become a death trap. Dogs do not sweat, but pant to breathe in cool air. When the air becomes as warm as the dog's body temperature, her body-cooling system fails and the dog can suffer brain damage, go into a coma, and rapidly die.

Speedy treatment is essential. Remove the dog to a cool place. Immerse her in a tub of water if possible, or wet her down with a garden hose or buckets of water. Wrap the dog in wet towels; add ice packs to the head, neck, and groin area if possible, *and get to a veterinarian immediately.*

Because puppies are so curious, they are prone to getting into any number of toxic substances, resulting in **poisoning**. These include houseplants, outdoor plants, household substances such cleaning products, pesticides, and medications, and other products such as paint thinner, kerosene, and so on. See chapter 3 for information about the ASPCA Animal Poison Control Center.

One of the most deadly substances is antifreeze, which tastes sweet to dogs. A few licks results in kidney damage. Only slightly more than that ends in death. Get veterinary help *at once*. There is no home treatment.

Aspirin is not toxic to dogs at doses recommended by a veterinarian (which are far below human doses), although it has been known to cause stomach irritation. It's best to give a dog a buffered or enteric-coated aspirin. *Tylenol, ibuprofen, and naproxen sodium are all toxic to dogs.*

Topical irritants must be washed off with a mild detergent. Never use substances such as turpentine to clean anything out of your dog's coat.

Some **topical irritants** that dogs get into include tar and grease, both of which can be safely removed by working vegetable or mineral oil into the coat and washing with a mild detergent. There's only one solution for getting rid of oil-based paint on a dog's coat—cut away the hair. Never use turpentine, kerosene, or gasoline to remove these substances. Just inhaling these harsh products causes pneumonia, which is life-threatening. (Signs of such inhalation include vomiting, tremors, convulsions, and coma.)

Porcupine quills are painful and usually end up in the dog's face, which makes them difficult and painful to remove. Since the dog will have to be sedated or anesthetized, removal calls for veterinary skill. If there are just one or two and you want to do it yourself, use pliers (preferably the needlenose type) placed close to the skin, and draw the quill out by the same path it went in. If even one breaks, it's off to the vet's for surgical removal.

The bane of every country or suburban dog owner is the small black and white **skunk.** A large can of plain tomato juice is an old standby—and it works—but if you use it on a dog with a long white coat, the dog will turn pink. A large dog will require several cans.

There are some new products on the market to eliminate skunk odor. You'll need to toss out the skunked collar and leash (remove ID or rabies tags first), because the smell will never go away. Shampoo and rinse the dog several times

Curious puppies will not have enough sense to stay away from things that can harm them. Be vigilant!

(preferably outdoors), following product directions. Some groomers and some veterinary hospitals offer this service. If you find one in your area that does, add them to your emergency phone numbers list!

Snakes and toads fascinate puppies by their slithery or erratic movement, but some varieties are dangerous playmates. Most snakes (even the ones that bite) are nonpoisonous and no cause for alarm; still, it pays to check on what your pup is playing with in the garden.

There are only four poisonous snake varieties in the United States: cottonmouths (aka water moccasins), copperheads, rattlesnakes, and coral snakes. One way to tell the difference (but only after the attack) is by the presence of fang marks, which are only seen in the bite of poisonous snakes—although this identification is lost on a densely coated dog. Your library is a good source of information (including color illustrations) of snakes, because it is seldom appropriate to get close enough to the head and mouth to see which type is confronting you or your dog!

The reaction to a bite is immediate and the symptoms are similar to those of other kinds of poisoning: panting, drooling, restlessness, weakness, and finally shock and even death. The bite of a coral snake results in excruciating pain, vomiting, diarrhea, convulsions, and coma. That is the worst-case scenario. The site of a bite from a poisonous snake (when you can locate it) shows rapid reaction, with swelling, redness, and extreme pain in the area.

Typical First-Aid Situations

When you notice anything unusual in the way your puppy is acting, ask yourself these questions:

What caused you to think there was a problem?
What was your first clue there was something wrong?
Is your puppy eating normally?
Does your puppy have a fever?
What do her stools look like?
Is your puppy limping?
When you do a hands-on exam, is she sore anywhere?
Can you feel a lump? Is anything red or swollen?

Write down anything you've noticed. When you call your veterinarian, be prepared to give specific details.

Because of the intense pain, the first thing to do is restrain the dog and get to the veterinarian *immediately*. Familiarize yourself with the snake-bite kit in your first-aid kit (it's in there!), because you will have to start treatment if it will take time to reach the vet. If it's possible to kill the snake, take the remains with you for positive identification.

Toads taste awful, so if your dog bites one, there will be frothing at the mouth and drooling. However, only one species of toad (Bufo) is poisonous. It is found in the southern United States. Death from a Bufo bite can occur in as little as fifteen minutes. Flush the dog's mouth, using a hose if possible, and induce vomiting by giving one to three teaspoons of hydrogen peroxide (3 percent) every ten minutes, or place one-half to one teaspoon of salt at the back of the tongue. *Get the dog to a vet!*

Life-Saving Procedures

There are three things you should know how to do that could save your dog's life. Artificial respiration may be required to get the dog breathing again, and heart massage is used when no heartbeat can be felt or heard. The Heimlich maneuver is used to dislodge a foreign object that is causing the dog to choke.

Artificial Respiration

The easiest way to administer artificial respiration is by compressing the chest. Here is the five-step method:

1. Feel or listen for a pulse or heartbeat.
2. Clear the mouth of secretions and foreign objects. (You might have to use the Heimlich maneuver to remove an obstruction that's out of reach.)
3. Lay the dog on her *right* side on a flat surface.
4. Place both hands on the chest and press down sharply, releasing immediately. (If you do *not* hear air going in and out, switch to the mouth-to-nose method below.)
5. Continue until the dog is breathing on her own, or as long as the heart is beating.

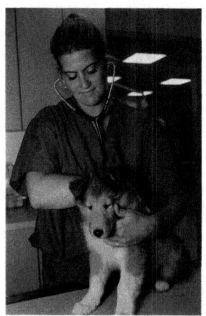

For the mouth-to-nose method:

1. Feel or listen for a pulse or heartbeat.
2. Clear the mouth of secretions and foreign objects. (You might have to use the Heimlich maneuver to remove an obstruction that's out of reach.)
3. Pull the tongue forward and keep the lips closed with your hand.
4. Take a breath and, with your mouth over the dog's nose, blow a steady stream of air for three seconds.
5. Release to let the air out. Continue until the dog is breathing on her own, or as long as the heart is beating.

Emergency treatment means you do what you can to aid and immobilize your dog, then get her to the vet right away.

Heart Massage

When heart massage is combined with mouth-to-nose resuscitation (it takes two people), it is called canine CPR (cardio-pulmonary resuscitation). Heart massage alone, however, also brings air to the lungs.

To perform heart massage, follow steps 1 and 2 above for artificial respiration, then, *for small dogs and puppies:*

3. Standing in back of the dog, place one hand on the sternum (bottom of chest) behind the dog's elbow with your thumb on top, fingers beneath.
4. With the other hand above your thumb, over the heart, press the chest firmly six times. Count to five (to let the chest expand) and repeat until the heart is beating or no heartbeat is felt for five minutes.

For *large dogs,* follow the same procedure but place the heel of your hand on the rib cage behind the elbow (which will be over the heart).

The Heimlich Maneuver

This is the method used to clear the dog's airway when she's choking. She'll be breathing hard, coughing, pawing at his mouth, and in a panic. Put one hand over her nose, pressing down on her lips with your thumb and forefinger. With your other hand, press down the lower jaw to pry her mouth open.

If you can't see anything or feel anything with a finger, lay the dog on her side and lower her head by putting a pillow under her hindquarters. On a puppy or small dog, place one hand a couple of inches below the bottom of her ribcage (the sternum) and the other hand on the dog's back for support. (On a larger dog, place both hands below the sternum.) Press *sharply* in and up. Repeat until the foreign object is dislodged. What you are doing is literally knocking the air out of her, so the object is expelled by the force of the air. If the dog is unconscious, do artificial respiration (after the object is removed, if possible) and immediately get going to the veterinarian.

Male and Female Problems

The Male

A normal male dog has two testicles descended into the scrotum by the age of 6 months. Before that, one or both testicles may go back up into the groin temporarily when the puppy is cold, playing, or otherwise excited. After 6 months, if only one testicle has descended into the scrotum the dog is called monorchid;

If you spay your girl before her first heat cycle, you virtually eliminate any chance of her getting mammary cancer.

if neither testicle is down, the dog is cryptorchid. The condition is of concern to breeders because it is an inherited defect. If this happens to your pet, check with your vet regarding neutering; the procedure will be just a little bit more complicated—but still safe and very important. It is helpful also to inform the breeder, who will use the information in planning future breedings.

Prostatitis occurs in unneutered males. Signs include fever and painful urination (even dripping pus), with the dog standing hunched up and in obvious discomfort. This infection is successfully treated with antibiotics. Once prostatitis is eliminated, having the dog neutered prevents a repeat infection. Have your dog neutered and you won't have to worry about him developing prostatitis.

The mature male normally has a small amount of white or yellowish discharge from the skin covering the penis, which the dog cleans himself. Excessive, darker discharge with a foul odor is a sign of **infection.** Your veterinarian will show you how to treat it.

The Female

Mammary gland tumors, half of which are malignant in female dogs, are virtually eliminated by having the bitch spayed before the onset of sexual maturity (or the first heat cycle), which normally occurs at about 6 months of age.

Pyometra is a very serious disease in which the uterus fills with pus. It is fatal if not promptly treated. It is also entirely preventable, as is cancer of the uterus, by having your bitch spayed.

The signs of **vaginitis** include excessive licking of the vulva in the bitch's effort to clean herself. The hair around the vulva may be stained. Another sign is painful urination. The infection is treated with antibiotics and douches.

Part III

Enjoying
Your Puppy

Chapter 7

Housetraining

Housetraining is sometimes called house*breaking*. It's easy to see how that word gets confused with all kinds of other things puppies do, none of which is what any owner of a new puppy has in mind! So "house*training*" it is, and it begins (as you read in chapter 4) the minute you walk in the door with your new puppy.

Preparations

Before you pick up the puppy, select a small area where you will want him to eliminate. This can be a small spot behind a bush in the garden, in one corner of the driveway, in a dog run set on crushed stone, or beside the curb in the city. As soon as you arrive home with the puppy, before you go indoors, take him *on leash* to that small area.

It is very important to select this one place and not confuse the puppy by going for a walk. It's also important to have him on one end of the leash with you on the other. During the training period, your puppy will learn that he is always taken to that exact same spot to go potty. Dogs relate to many things by their sense of smell and by touch. After relieving himself in that one area a couple of times, he'll know by the scent and how it feels under his feet that he's in the right place. (It's up to you to pick up after the pup, by the way! Don't worry; the scent will remain.)

After a few successful trips, you can add a command word, such as "Go potty" or whatever one-word term you wish, as you reach the spot. You'll get plenty of practice—at 8 to 10 weeks, puppies need to eliminate about every two hours.

After he's gone potty, it's time for play—off-lead if your yard is fenced.

The Crate

Now is the prime time for using a crate. This essential piece of canine equipment is described in chapter 4. Housetraining begins and ends with the crate. Call it a crate or a bed or a den, but not a cage (that's a four-letter word); it is your pup's home at home or away, his refuge in times of stress (yours or his), and an ideal spot for his undisturbed nap. As you'll see, it is also an invaluable tool for housetraining.

The kitchen is the area you are most likely to have chosen for your puppy's confinement, so during the day that is where you should put the crate. Pick a spot in the kitchen that is accessible to you and the puppy and leave the crate door

This Collie cannot get into trouble in his crate.

open so that the pup can go in and out. When you want him to stay put, close the door. At night, you can move the crate into your bedroom if you like, or indulge yourself and buy two crates. You could end up with three—a third one for the car—so you'd never have to move any of them!

So you already have the crate and, if needed, the exercise pen and pet gates for doorways leading anywhere you don't want the puppy to be. Here are some other items you'll need to have on hand.

Newspapers and/or Training Pads

Your puppy must have somewhere to go potty when you aren't Johnny-on-the-spot. Put two or three layers of newspaper at one end of the exercise pen or in one corner of his confined area. (Do not paper the entire floor!) If your supply does not meet the demand, you can always ask a neighbor to save papers for you. Training pads are available at pet supply stores or by catalogue. Most are made with a plastic backing to protect wood floors and are treated with a scent to attract the pup and also to eliminate odors after use.

Both newspapers and pads are intended only to prevent accidents from happening all over the place. When the puppy uses them, make no comment at

If you will not be available to take your puppy outdoors every hour or two, starting him off with newspapers can be useful.

The Dog's Senses

The dog's eyes are designed so that he can see well in relative darkness, has excellent peripheral vision, and is very good at tracking moving objects—all skills that are important to a carnivore. Dogs also have good depth perception. Those advantages come at a price, though: Dogs are nearsighted and are slow to change the focus of their vision. It's a myth that dogs are colorblind. However, while they can see some (but not all) colors, their eyes were designed to most clearly perceive subtle shades of gray—an advantage when they are hunting in low light.

Dogs have about six times fewer taste buds on their tongue than humans do. They can taste sweet, sour, bitter, and salty tastes, but with so few taste buds it's likely that their sense of taste is not very refined.

A dog's ears can swivel independently, like radar dishes, to pick up sounds and pinpoint their location. Dogs can locate a sound in $6/100$ of a second and hear sound four times farther away than we can (which is why there is no reason to yell at your dog). They can also hear sounds at far higher pitches than we can.

In their first few days of life, puppies primarily use their sense of touch to navigate their world. Whiskers on the face, above the eyes, and below the jaws are sensitive enough to detect changes in airflow. Dogs also have touch-sensitive nerve endings all over their bodies, including on their paws.

Smell may be a dog's most remarkable sense. Dogs have about 220 million scent receptors in their nose, compared to about 5 million in humans, and a large part of the canine brain is devoted to interpreting scent. Not only can dogs smell scents that are very faint, but they can also accurately distinguish between those scents. In other words, when you smell a pot of spaghetti sauce cooking, your dog probably smells tomatoes and onions and garlic and oregano and whatever else is in the pot.

all—no "good" or "bad" puppy, and no sign of frustration or anger. Afterward, put him in his crate and discard the papers. Clean up with an enzyme deodorizer (available at pet supply stores), and put down fresh newspapers or a new pad. The pup's acute sense of smell will lead him back to where he eliminated, so a cleaner made for this purpose is essential.

By the way, using newspapers for housetraining will not—I repeat, will *not*—prompt your puppy to go on the newspapers that just fell off the sofa. Besides, if he's near the sofa, someone is watching him, right?

Poop Clean-up Tools

Poop-scoops for cleaning up outdoors come in different styles and sizes. Try them out in the store to see which one you like best. The size will depend on the adult size of your dog since these metal tools last a dog's lifetime.

You'll also need pick-ups to have in your pocket on every walk. For small breeds and very small pups, fold-top sandwich bags work well, but your pet supply store will have a variety of plastic mitts for dogs of all sizes. All of them work the same way: Put your hand inside the bag or mitt, pick up the poop, and fold the plastic down over it. Close it with a twist-tie and drop it in the trash. Quick, easy, and sanitary.

Establishing Rules

Each and every person in the family is involved in housetraining the puppy and needs to understand the how and why of the rules for housetraining. On leash is the first answer to *how*. You are not taking the puppy for a walk. Walks come later. Consider this a "business trip." Take him to his special spot and stand there. No chitchat. Pretend to not even look at him. Occasionally a pup will decide to sit while you stand (they know more obedience stuff than you think!).

> **TIP**
>
> Keep a record of the time the puppy went out, how long the trip lasted, and whether he urinated, defecated, or did both. Soon you will see a pattern emerge that will help you anticipate his potty needs. Use the "Puppy's Potty Schedule" table on page 105 to chart his habits over the course of a week.

If that happens, just take a few steps this way and that to get him moving so that he will pick up the scent and be encouraged to go. This part takes time, but it's time well spent.

As to *why* the leash, there are several reasons. For starters, the leash prevents the puppy from taking off on a game of chase-me. The major reason, however, is that the leash keeps *you* beside the puppy so that you can say "good dog" *as* he eliminates. Food rewards are totally inappropriate. All the puppy needs is your calm approval *as* he's taking care of business.

I cannot repeat this often enough: The timing of everything you say or do to a puppy—whether it is praise, a preventive warning, or a correction— must be done *as that specific action occurs.* In this case, praising the pup after he has relieved himself only tells him that you approve of whatever he is doing *at that precise moment,* which could be straining on his leash, jumping, or barking. Obviously, that's not what you were praising him for when you said "good dog"!

Indoor Rules

When you come back indoors, don't make the common mistake of letting the puppy run free all over your house. That kind of freedom means only one thing: freedom to get into trouble resulting in freedom to be punished, because puppies on their own *will* get into trouble. Be kind to your puppy. Confining him to his one room or area is for his safety.

What goes in must come out. When you set your dog on a regular schedule of meals, you'll be able to fig-ure out when he needs to eliminate.

Rules #1, #2, #3, and #4: Keep an eye on your puppy!

If need be, he can go into his crate with a toy. He will probably curl up and go to sleep. Puppies need a lot of sleep because they are growing so fast.

After a nap, your puppy will need to go outside to eliminate—immediately. Take advantage of this urgent need and teach him the word you've chosen for it. "You have to go *outside? Outside?*" (or "go potty," said as one word, of course). Bear in mind that after the puppy urinates, he will have to defecate, so don't return to the house too quickly. Did you know that it is normal for an adult dog to have up to four to six bowel movements a day, and that puppies can have two within a few minutes? Be sure that he has finished and you'll have prevented an accident.

Stick to the Schedule

Remember the rules:

- Patience—for all that standing around during a potty break.
- Consistency—the same words, the same tone of voice, the same place every time.
- Timing—perfect, precise, on-target timing is your key to success.

Here's an approximate schedule for successful housetraining. It's approximate due to your individual puppy's age, his previous training, if any, and your own normal daily routine.

First thing in the morning (6 or 7 a.m.)   Expect early rising for the first couple of weeks (6 or 6:30 a.m.), until the puppy gets into the family's routine. At the first sound, or before, snap on the leash and get your puppy to his potty spot fast!

Puppy's Potty Schedule

	Mon	Tues	Wed	Thurs	Fri	Sat	Sun
7 a.m.							
8 a.m.							
9 a.m.							
10 a.m.							
11 a.m.							
Noon							
1 p.m.							
2 p.m.							
3 p.m.							
4 p.m.							
5 p.m.							
6 p.m.							
7 p.m.							
8 p.m.							
9 p.m.							
10 p.m.							

When you come in, he'll be full of energy even if you aren't, so be sure he has fresh water and let him play while you fix your own breakfast. Put down newspapers, if needed.

Food   Put his food down and say "good *come*" as he runs toward you. Wait fifteen or twenty minutes and then take him out for a potty break.

Play   If it's a nice day and you have a few minutes, now is a good time to play a game of chase-me or to play with a toy, off-lead if your fencing is secure. If it isn't, or if you live in the city, playtime will be back indoors in a room other than the one in which he is confined.

Follow this with another potty trip, and then it's time for a rest! He can curl up in his crate, where he will be fast asleep for a couple of hours.

Then it's the same routine: on leash outside, followed by playtime, followed by food, water, another nap, and then—surprise—go potty again! That's how a busy puppy's day goes. By making a note of each time he defecates, you'll see a

Stay a step ahead of accidents by making sure that your dog is confined in areas that are easily cleaned.

Puppies usually have to eliminate soon after they wake up.

pattern develop, and that will enable you to watch for, and spot, the telltale circling, whining, or pawing that precedes his need to go potty.

If you're too late, or almost too late, give him the *"aacht!"* command. If he's small enough to carry, get him out the door and snap on the leash as you go or when you get there. Otherwise, you'll have to chalk it up to human error—your fault, not his.

As the amount you feed decreases and the meals are cut from three to two, and as the ability of your puppy to control bodily functions increases, the fewer trips outside he'll need. It is the noonday meal that is eliminated at any time from 6 months to 1 year. Check with your veterinarian. Often it is the puppy who suddenly loses interest in the midday meal, but some chowhounds will eat whatever whenever. Obesity can be avoided.

The final meal of the day comes at 5 p.m. and is followed, as always, by a trip to go potty. Crating the puppy while the family has dinner is a good idea. It's the first step in training him not to beg when people are eating. (Later, when he's all grown up, he can go either into his crate or to a designated spot for an obedient Long-Down.)

Keep in mind that puppies are not isolationists. They are pack animals, and their need for company is very real. After dinner, when everyone is apt to be home from work and school, is a good time for your puppy to socialize with the family. Be alert for any go-potty signals as well as the investigation of things that are out-of-bounds, but encourage play, handling, petting, and—naturally—cuddling! For a rambunctious puppy, attaching a twelve-inch piece of old leash or rope to his collar will give you the means to calm the activity. And, you guessed it, another potty break after all this fun!

Offer a final drink of water for the day around 8 p.m. and pick up the water bowl.

At 10 p.m., take the puppy for his last trip to go potty. Then it's into his crate with a small "good-night, good-dog" biscuit.

If you decide to have the crate in your bedroom overnight, place it in a corner where it will be out of your way and turned (or covered) so that he can't watch you or the television. If you have the TV on, keep the sound low. There are a couple of downsides to this nighttime plan:

- The puppy may sleep while you're reading or watching television and start fussing when the lights go out. (You can try a very sharp "No!" and then ignore any further whining.)
- There's a chance that the simple sound of your turning over in bed at 3 a.m. will waken the puppy, who will need to go potty yet again!

Left in the kitchen, chances are good that he'll sleep through the night—unless, of course, you have midnight fridge-raiders in the family. Make it out of bounds for them until the puppy is accustomed to sleeping through the night.

Playtime comes only after potty time during trips outdoors.

> ## Tips for City Dogs
>
> Carry a small puppy in the elevator and up and down stairs. A puppy too big to carry is still a puppy, so protect him in the elevator by letting him sit in the corner with you standing in front of him so that he won't get stepped on.
>
> Keep your coat and the leash handy. First thing in the morning can be very early!
>
> City street noises can be frightening to a puppy. Find as secluded a spot as possible in which to curb your pup. Take plastic baggies with you and do your part to keep your city clean.

When the puppy has learned how to let you know that he has to go out, you can begin to let him outside on his own (only in a fenced-in area), but watch from a window if possible to be certain he visits his potty spot. Promote him too soon and your clever puppy will diddle you by playing around outdoors, barking to be let in—and promptly having an accident on your best carpet. Again, your fault, not his. Products made to clean pet stains remove the odor. Household detergents and carpet cleaners won't do it. Unless you remove every trace of the scent, your puppy will return to have an accident in the same spot indoors over and over again, just as he does outside.

Remember the *"as"* rule. Don't scold a puppy for having had an accident. It's past tense. It's up to you to prevent accidents and also to accept the fact that you are only human and you can't prevent everything!

Paper Training

If everyone leaves the house in the morning and returns six to eight hours later, you have several options. You can ask a friend, neighbor, or professional pet sitter to take your puppy out of his confined area for an hour or so in the middle of the day to go potty, play with him, feed him, and take him out again before returning him to the confined area. Or you can paper-train.

Leave several thicknesses of newspaper in one corner of the area to which the puppy is confined when you are out—in one corner of an exercise pen away from his water dish and bed, or in a corner by the back door, for example.

Be patient with your pup, and soon enough he'll be housetrained and reliable.

Warning: If you paper the entire floor (or even too large an area), the puppy will use the entire area and go on to turn at least half of it into confetti. Boredom has a way of expressing itself.

On your return, take the puppy outside as usual and clean up the newspapers in silence. That gives the pup the message that what he did is okay, but only okay, nothing to warrant either praise or disapproval.

When the puppy has not used the newspapers for some time, you can gradually diminish the size of the papered area. However, many people who must leave their adult dogs alone all day routinely put newspapers down, just in case. Better a soiled newspaper than a damaged bladder. (Cheaper, too.)

Toy breeds can be trained to use litter boxes made especially for small dogs without the "privacy" cover that kitties prefer. These litter boxes contain specially treated pebbles rather than the conventional cat litter. (Cat litter creates a sandstorm when the dog kicks with his back feet or when a long-coated dog shakes.) When the dog is no longer confined, the litter box is often put in the corner of a bathroom, laundry room, or other out-of-the-way place to which the dog has easy access. Or you can stick with paper training.

When Is the Puppy Housetrained?

When your puppy has been accident-free for several days, you're on your way. When the puppy has been clean for a couple of months and routinely asks to be taken out, congratulations; you are just about there. But keep in mind that your puppy cannot have perfect control at all times under all circumstances. Some puppies still have an occasional accident between age 6 months and a year—one more reason to confine your puppy when you can't be there to supervise him.

Now you'll be taking the puppy for walks, visits, obedience classes, and just about anywhere you can show him off. Take two things with you: pick-up bags or mitts and a few small treats to reward perfect behavior away from home.

Forming Good Habits

Puppies get away with doing things that are totally unacceptable for an adult dog. It may be cute to have your little puppy pouncing at your knees when you come home, but when he's a full-grown 140-pound Newfoundland, he'll knock you flat! Teach the young puppy right from the get-go the good manners you will want in your adult dog, and remember that the command is "off" (*not* "get down" or "no jumping"—just "OFF!").

Puppies of this age should be kept off the furniture for two long-term reasons. First, chairs, couches, and beds are for people. Dogs have their own furniture, which is kept on the floor. Second, and just as important, puppies are apt to make Superman leaps *off* furniture, which can permanently damage the growth plates in their legs—something that can't be seen until the deformity is visible months later.

For this reason, too, don't try to force reluctant young pups to go down steps. Teach Rufus how to do it when he is physically ready. If you want to see how scary going down stairs can be for a little puppy, go to the top of the steps, get down on all fours yourself, and have a good look. Now, think about how safe *you'd* feel about going down!

> ### Your Dog's "Human" Age
>
> There are several ways of comparing dog years to human years, but here is a modern one: One dog year equals fifteen human years; two dog years equals twenty-four human years. Then add four years to the human's life for every one of the dog's (three dog years equals twenty-eight human years, four equals thirty-two, five equals thirty-six, and so on).
>
> Another factor regarding age is size. Small dogs live longer (eighteen to twenty years is not uncommon), while giant breeds (Great Danes, Irish Wolfhounds) live only five to ten years.

Puppy's First Playtime

When the puppy's immunizations have taken effect, you can venture further afield than your own backyard. Short walks and playtime in different environments are good for exercise and for socializing. These excursions will also teach you to pick up after your dog! It's the law in some places, and just plain responsible dog ownership everywhere else.

Play on a beach or a stroll in the park will be full of learning experiences for a young puppy. The retractable leash is perfect for these play-walks, because it extends to give the puppy about sixteen feet of freedom, controlled by you.

Fifteen to twenty minutes total time is enough at first. Add a few more minutes every few days, but don't overdo it. Exercise also depends on the weather. Hazy, hot, and humid is not the time for outdoor walks or playtime. Icy pavements or streets may contain chemical melting agents, which must be washed off as soon as you get home.

Chapter 8

Training Your Puppy

Y ou began training your puppy when you took her in your arms and said, "Yes! This one's for me!" All the way home she listened to every word you said and how you said it. And, as you carried or led her through the door into your home, you clearly indicated to your puppy one of two things: *Here you are, puppy, it's all yours!* or *Welcome, puppy, to our home!* Either you turned her loose to fend for herself or you began teaching her how to become part of the family.

All of which is another way of saying that training your puppy does not only refer to obedience classes with an instructor to guide you. Basic training does not wait until your puppy is 6 months old. It begins immediately. You are teaching the pup, intentionally or not, what she's allowed to do—and thereby earn your smiles and sweet talk—and what she is definitely not allowed to do. A puppy is a sponge, and spends every waking moment soaking up her environment and figuring out how all of it relates to *her*. (Puppies, like kids, are very "me" oriented.) Every dog needs to know her exact place within her new family circle.

Puppies use the self-teaching method if no one tells them otherwise. A pup learns to read canine body language from her mother and littermates. She learns by doing, and evaluating the consequences *as* she is doing it. Let's say Mimi bites a littermate's ear. The other pup screams and bites back. "Hmmm," thinks Mimi, "he didn't like that," and she may try it again to find out how hard a bite is okay. If her second bite is too hard, Mom gets into the act and pins Mimi to the floor by the neck, which is her way of saying "Cut it out—*now*."

Mimi gets the message that biting hard will not be tolerated. It is her first lesson in bite inhibition. However, once is never enough and she will try it again.

Puppies need consistent and constant reminders. Bite inhibition happens to be one of the most important lessons to be learned.

Now it is your turn to act with prompt intervention. To be successful, your action must be the smallest correction necessary to end the undesirable behavior and to teach what is acceptable. Note that a "correction" does not necessarily mean punishment, and it does not merely stop the misconduct. A correction always ends by having the puppy do something—anything—for which you can say "good dog." Your motto will be: *Teach, don't punish.*

Consistency

There are three basic training ingredients you need to turn your puppy into an intelligent, well-behaved, cooperative dog. They are confinement, prevention, and consistency. (There are more, but this is the foundation.) We discussed confinement and prevention in chapter 4. Now let's look at consistency.

Everyone in your family will need to consistently use the same commands with the pup and consistently enforce the same house rules.

Your puppy hasn't yet completely learned her own canine language, and you're already teaching her a foreign one, so you must be consistent. Use *exactly* the same word to mean *exactly* the same thing every time to enable the puppy to make a clear connection between the word and the desired action. Pretend she speaks a rare dialect—you can't *punish* her for not understanding what you said!

Here's the standard example of how this works using the word "off." You'll be using it as a one-word command, which your pup will learn easily if you are consistent and don't confuse her. Use "off" when you mean *Don't jump up on Aunt Martha.* Also when you mean *Get off the couch!* And it can mean *Don't put your paws on the windowsill.* But it is a *one-word* command. Your puppy will be confused (*not* disobedient) if you say "don't jump up," one time, "get off" another, "get down" on another occasion, and "stay off" still another.

Looking ahead, how will Mimi know what you want her to do when you are trying to teach the commands "down" and "stay," which have nothing to do with "off"? All you have taught her is that sometimes you don't know what you're talking about! So, it is *one* word for *each* action. When you want to convey clearly to Mimi any form of "remove yourself," the word to use is "off."

Think how quickly your puppy learned her name. That's because it is one word and you use it consistently. Okay, so sometimes you add a few endearing adjectives, but mostly, it's "Mimi" this and "Mimi" that. Get into the habit of using one-word commands consistently and Mimi will be speaking your language in no time.

Consistency is everything in the life of a dog. Older dogs can adjust when we change routines, but puppies thrive on knowing what to expect and when to expect it. Consistency makes you a reliable, trustworthy person. Trust is of prime importance to your puppy. If she trusts you, she will listen and learn from you.

Puppy Learning

An obedient, loving, fun companion is not difficult to achieve through home training. From 3 to 6 months of age the puppy is learning *how* to learn, so training sessions are tied in with fun, simply paying attention, praise, and being with you. Discipline from you instills *self*-discipline and *self*-confidence, but puppies this age are still emotionally immature and most are sensitive to correction. Some will remain that way. Never make a harsh correction or punishment with your hand, voice, or leash. (Remember the language barrier: Make yourself clear, and don't punish your pup for not understanding what you said!)

At this age all puppies are more or less equal in everything but size. They all have the same very short attention spans, some are a bit shy, some more bold, but all are curious.

There are six standard commands every dog should know: heel, come, sit, stand, stay, and down. With a new puppy, it doesn't matter too much where you begin. The important thing is to practice every day at various times throughout the day, and never to be in any hurry to move ahead to the next lesson. You do not set the pace for learning, Mimi does.

Training sessions should last only two to five minutes, which is approximately the length of your pup's attention span. If you push her longer than that, she will stop paying attention to you. Don't start a training session immediately after the pup has eaten because she'll be sleepy. However, you should practice at odd times throughout the day, even if all you get is a three-second "sit" or "stay." Your pup will love the attention and your praise.

Motivation for a puppy lies in her desire to please you. You may find your puppy offering up behaviors before you even ask for them.

This is FUN stuff! (You may need to repeat that ten times to remind yourself.) End every session with a near-perfect performance. That could be one two-second sit, or three little heeling steps next to you. Tell her how "perfect" it was. Lay it on! *Really* let her know how pleased you are that she got it right.

Rewards

Motivation for a puppy to do anything at all lies first in her desire to please you. Realistically, treats run a close second. Regular dog biscuits do not make good training treats because they take too long to chew. Tiny bits of plain cheese are good taste treats, as are one or two Cheerios (which are also easier to keep in your pocket). A thin slice of hot dog will perk up the interest of almost any dog who is not concentrating. But don't overdo the treats!

Rewards come in three forms: treats, pats, and verbal praise. To grade your student's qualification for a reward, consider a treat the equivalent of an A, a pat a B, and verbal praise a C. Any two together equal an A+, so be very careful not to go overboard or you'll run out of appropriate compensation and your puppy will quit school!

Verbal praise has a range from ecstatic (for the first few correct responses from a very young pup) to a calm "good dog" as Mimi grows up and becomes more expert. *Don't* overuse treats when practicing. As you get a quick correct response to each word command, gradually cut back on the treats and substitute "good dog" or just a big smile. (An A+ will retain its impact all the way through college, as will ecstatic praise.)

Dog Talk

What you say to a puppy and how you say it can determine how quickly she learns. All human conversation is perceived by the dog as meaningless sound. Try this: In the midst of some long-winded chit-chat, say your dog's name emphatically and watch her take notice. When using the one-word training commands, remember that lesson. Her name gives you her attention; one word tells her what to do. It is "Mimi, SIT"—loud and clear. Never "Mimi, Sit. Sit. Sit. Mimi, you're not listening—I said Sit. *SIT, Mimi!*" That is called *nagging*, and Mimi will tune you out. The puppy is not being disobedient or stubborn. She's just confused—totally! Avoid sounding like a drill sergeant. Smile, speak clearly, and let the dog do the barking.

Teaching "Heel"

Heeling is not the same as going for a walk. No smelling the flowers, no lifting a leg on every hydrant. Heeling is an obedience exercise in which the dog stays close beside you at your left side, paying attention only to you and where you are going.

As your puppy grows up, heeling will become the safe way for you to walk your dog through crowds and across streets with her ignoring all normal and unusual distractions. It is the easiest lesson to begin with, because you'll be taking your new puppy outside on leash to eliminate and you can practice three times on each trip—on your way out, after she relieves herself, and while coming back inside.

This will not be the heeling exercise as done in obedience class, but more of a lesson in "pre-heeling" because you can begin off-leash anywhere that's safe, indoors or out. And instead of "heel," you can use the friendlier "let's go!"

Begin by getting the pup's attention *as* she's trotting along next to you, to make her conscious of what she is doing. Some pups will follow if you lean over, quietly clapping your hands in front of their nose, some like to hear cheerful chatter, others just want to go wherever you go. As you move along, you can add an occasional "Mimi, watch me!" (No doubt by now you've noticed that some "one-word" commands are actually two or three words. Just run them together and your puppy will catch on perfectly.)

Now it's time to try this with Mimi on a leash. Keep the puppy on your left side (a must when you go to class). Before you begin, have her sit. Then step forward with your left foot *as* you say "let's go" or "heel." You want the puppy to learn to move forward only when your left leg moves. Memorize the phrase "lead with the left" and you won't confuse your puppy. If you step forward with your right leg, it means Mimi has to stay.

Hold her attention by walking just quickly enough to make the puppy want to keep up with you. It all begins with just one step in the right direction (with the left leg), followed by verbal praise. If she's not paying attention, stop and begin again. *No correction.* Following a treat that smells good may get her motivated, but if a young pup's attention is totally elsewhere, this is not the right moment for a lesson. A few minutes of playtime, followed by a drink of water, may put her back on track to try again. If not, give it a rest for now.

Practicing

You can practice anywhere, any time, on or off leash. *As* you notice Mimi walking next to you—from fridge to stove, across the room, etc.—take advantage of the opportunity to get in a speedy "let's go!—good dog." Be realistic in what you expect of a puppy. A few steps on command earn a verbal reward. A few more steps earn a small treat reward. A week later Mimi is heeling nicely? Praise and stop practicing immediately! Practice again later.

Puppies arrive in the winter, too, when outside lessons are not possible. A long hallway or a basement is perfect for indoor heel training. There are no distractions and space is limited, so Mimi can't go too far wrong, and you're sure to have her attention because *you* are the most fascinating thing around.

Add some right turns for variety and to be sure she's really paying attention. *As* you make the turn, bend over and lead with your hand to keep her on course. Left turns are harder because *you* have more to do. Put your left foot in front of the pup to gently guide her into the turn. Careful, or you'll step on the pup and she won't think this game is much fun! However, if your left foot happens to bump the puppy or she plows into it, don't apologize. If she thinks it was her mistake, she'll learn to pay closer attention.

If at First You Don't Succeed . . .

If you don't get the desired result from this or any other lesson, you just didn't explain it in a way the pup could understand, so try again. And again. And again! (Come on! How are you doing with that rare language dialect?) Keep your sense of humor.

Puppies learn by consistent, patient repetition. If the pup gives up trying and you physically put her in the desired position for any of these training exercises, it destroys her self-confidence and the pup will begin to wait for your intervention. Puppies also give up if their efforts always end in punishment or your obvious disapproval. It's called learned helplessness. As much as possible, let the puppy perform on her own. If you ignore her errors and put the emphasis on her successes, Mimi will learn quickly.

Teaching "Sit"

The "sit" command is an easy way to have your puppy show off her good manners. Mimi can sit when Aunt Martha comes visiting, when you meet a friend (especially a small child) out walking, when you are preparing her dinner, when she has to wait for just about anything from a dog biscuit to her turn in the pool. It is also one of the easiest exercises to practice, because you can ask her to sit whenever and wherever you like. A sit is especially good for little everyday things, like having her leash attached.

The command is "Mimi, *sit.*" You may have noticed that all commands are preceded by the dog's name; that's to get the pup's attention so she knows you aren't talking to Johnny or Mary. Puppies are proud to have a name. It's when they reach adolescence (the terrible teens) that they, like other teenagers we all

Learning "sit" is easy, and will give both you and your pup a quick sense of accomplishment.

know, pretend they don't hear you. You can skip using her name any time you see the puppy about to sit. Quickly say "*sit*—good dog." Or if she is already sitting nicely, give her a "good sit" verbal reward.

The easiest way to teach a young pup to sit is to get her attention with a treat in your right hand when she's standing. Hold it in front of and just above her nose to make her look up. Then slowly move the treat backward over her head. Because Mimi wants to keep an eye on the goodie, her backside will have to drop to the floor. It takes a little practice (on your part, too) but it's a tried and true means of getting an unforced sit. *As* she assumes the position, give the command "Mimi—*sit*" and hand out the tiny treat. That's motivational teaching. The puppy performs the desired action by herself.

> ### T I P
>
> #### Release
>
> When the puppy is learning each command, it is important to teach her how you will release her from remaining in that position forever. The usual release is a simple "okay!" while clapping your hands to regain the dog's attention. (Even puppies like applause.) Now's the time to love her up and tell her how utterly fabulous she is.

Another way is to have the pup beside you (at your left side), and hold a treat in your right hand so she looks up. Then gently press down on her hindquarters with your left hand. With a large pup, you could put your left arm around her hindquarters and, with a gentle forward motion, bend her knees, forcing the sit. And, as you are coping with all that, brightly say "Mimi, *sit*." Confusing? You were warned! The motivational sit is easier.

If you followed the first method and Mimi is doing a prompt sit every time you give the command, you will soon graduate to using just the hand signal—making the same upward motion with your right hand, palm up as you did in raising the treat over her head—and the pup will do a very nice sit. Tricks or treats, anyone?

Teaching "Sit-Stay"

Once the puppy is able to sit still for a few seconds *every* time you ask her, you can begin to add "stay." A sit-stay of two or three seconds in the beginning is fine. When you reach twenty to thirty seconds, you can put her in a sit-stay and move one step away *on your right foot*. Stand almost toe to toe with the pup until she gets the idea that you mean she has to remain sitting until she hears the magic word, "okay."

Add to the distance between you *only* as Mimi is able to hold the sit-stay. The object is to have her obey you, not to see how long she can stay put. It may take weeks to work up to a thirty-second stay. Puppies are squirmy!

Teaching "Come"

The biggest, the *number one* mistake people make with this command is to say "Mimi, come" when there is no possible way to enforce it. Remember consistency? The puppy only has to disobey a few times when she hears "Mimi, come!" and you have *taught* her (and she has learned) that she has an option. She can come, or not. *Never* give her that choice. Only call "come" if the puppy is on her way into your outstretched arms, or on a leash so you can guide her toward you. That rule is in effect until your adult dog is "proofed" (tested by numerous and diverse distractions) at two years of age. And to be honest, with lots of dogs, it's a lifetime rule.

The second biggest mistake is to call the puppy to come to you in order to scold her. That's a people no-no. Children are sometimes guilty of doing this, so be sure they understand they must never do it to their puppy. If you catch Mimi being naughty, *you* go to her. (If you come upon the scene of a crime even one minute later, it's too late to scold or punish a dog.) Just never say "Mimi, come" if you are angry or impatient. The tone of your voice will tell her *not* to come, not to come anywhere near you; you have set her up to disobey you.

And if Mimi hears her name called for a detested nail trim or to come in from outdoors just when she's having fun or enjoying a nap, she soon learns it is not a perfect world. Dogs are not stupid! Why come when it means the good times are over?

So say "Mimi, come" when she is happily trotting toward you, or

Always call your puppy to come to you for something good and she will always come when you call.

when you have her on a leash a few feet in front of you and can guide her to you if she is distracted. Until she is older and much better educated, call the puppy using *only* her name when you can't enforce the "come." When she responds and is racing toward you, *then* get in a "Mimi, *come*—good dog" as quickly as you can say it.

Always use a happy voice, crouch down, open your arms wide, smile—and when Mimi is on her way, say "come!" If you've been having trouble getting a prompt response, have a treat ready for the big reunion.

Another way to encourage a puppy to come to you is to pretend to run the other way. It's the irresistible game of chase, and puppies love it! As the pup comes after you, stop, turn, and say "come!" (then smile, treat, or pat). Admittedly, you have to be somewhat agile.

"Come" is one of the primary safety signals, and therefore your goal must be 100 percent compliance. In any type of emergency involving you or your dog, you must be able to rely on A+ obedience for "come" and "stay." (Straight A's will do for responses to the other requests!)

Teaching "Leave It"

Before we get to the final elementary command (stand), there is one more your puppy needs to learn for her own protection, and that's the safety command "leave it." You're out for a walk and puppy comes upon roadkill or some carelessly discarded garbage. For the sake of your pup's health, you command "leave it!" (in a stern voice) and you will need to enforce it with a quick snap-and-release of the leash. If your pup doesn't hear (or understand) the "leave it" command, get her attention with *"aacht!"* followed by "leave it." (That's pronounced as one word, by the way.)

This command is so important that at 4 to 6 months of age you can even use entrapment as a teaching tool. When the puppy can't see you do it, plant a piece of trash, maybe an empty cereal box, on the floor and stick around until the pup goes to investigate. *As* she goes to sniff it, shout "leave it!" and *as* she retreats at the force of your voice, say "good dog" or "good leave it."

On your walks, you can use this command if the pup has ideas of tasting your neighbor's tulips, or at home if she has in mind to sample the goodies on the coffee table or help herself to the popcorn. Vary the emphasis you put on it, because it is an extremely versatile and useful command. It also has an amusing side effect. Many young puppies respond to the extreme urgency in your voice and not only "leave it" but do an instant down—flat on the ground!

"Leave it" is a useful command in a wide variety of situations.

Teaching "Stand"

When you give a dog any command, you have automatically assumed a dominant role and put the dog in a submissive one. Standing is a somewhat dominant canine posture, while sit and down are submissive canine positions, so it is sometimes difficult to teach a naturally submissive puppy to stand when told. Given the command "stand," many dogs will obey, but quickly lower their tails, ears, and head—all submissive body language. Be gentle and patient. In a perfect "stand," the puppy has four feet on the ground (that's the hard part), but it's also nice to see the head up and the tail wagging. Don't worry if at first your puppy would rather be a clown than stand still. Eventually they all grow up.

Mimi is learning the command "stay," which (fortunately, in this case) sounds a little like "stand." Whenever you catch her standing still, use it to your advantage. The puppy may pause for a moment to figure out which one you said, giving you the perfect opportunity to reinforce it with a "good *stand.*" Drag out the *a* and hit the *d*—"staaan-duh."

However, puppies do not spend much time standing around, so you'll have to teach her, not just rely on trying to catch her in the act. One way is to walk her into a stand. When she's pretty good at heeling, slow down and, as you come to a stop, bring your right hand in front of her (palm side toward her nose) *as* you say "stand." Perform this hand signal gently or Mimi will think she's going to be bonked and she'll duck!

Practice by taking one or two slow steps (on your right foot, without a "let's go" command) followed by a "stand" command. Getting that head held high and happy and the tail wagging calls for a treat, held waist-high and popped into the pup's mouth *as* you say "good stand." (If you don't work quickly, the pup will jump up to get the treat and the whole lesson will go down the drain!) In the early days of training, a couple of reasonably good "stands" are followed by a rousing romp. Standing still is *very hard.*

Make training practice part of your everyday interaction with your dog.

Again, take advantage of every possible occasion to ask your puppy to stand. If you've been asking her to sit before putting her dinner on the floor, now you can alternate "sit" with "stand"—and offer a treat reward right out of the dinner bowl.

Use the stand command to begin a grooming session, but release her after a few seconds. A perfect stand is only required of an adult dog for about a minute. Standing is necessary for at least part of her weekly grooming, but not standing at attention. In fact, during every grooming session you can make use of the sit, the stand, and the down. What a clever, cooperative puppy!

Teaching "Down"

Now we're talking total submission! Down is as low as you can get, and it is difficult for some puppies to accept. What is called the "dominant down"—a forced positioning of the puppy on her side with your hand on her neck and shoulder area—is restraint, not teaching. If your puppy is off-the-wall rambunctious and you are losing control, the dominant down is one method of regaining it—but never in anger, and always firmly but gently.

The drawback is you can get yourself into a wrestling match—and come out the loser. Placing your hands on the puppy's shoulders and calmly saying "settle" is a preferable, less combative method. Remember the rule: Let the dog perform the desired action by herself.

With Mimi doing a B+ sit-stay, hold a treat in the fingers of your right hand (let her sniff it or see it), run that hand in front of her nose, down at an angle, and out toward your feet. Be prepared to use your left hand on her shoulders *only* if necessary to guide her into the down position, which is flat on her tummy with front legs flat out in front. Deliver the treat *and* a "good *down!*" and release. Reinforce it by saying "good *down*" every time you catch her lying on the floor with a toy—or watching TV.

When the puppy can do a down all by herself in response to "Mimi, down," you can intermittently skip the treat, begin to add a "stay," and gradually—very gradually—work up to a down of one minute. As she matures, she'll be able to stay down for five minutes (or more if necessary), but even one minute is an eternity for an active pup, and you need to remain within a foot or two to start the exercise over again if she gets up.

It can't be emphasized enough: Go slowly—one step at a time—in all puppy training. If she did it right the first time, chalk it up to beginner's luck (hers and yours!). Without steady repetition, she will forget it just as quickly. It takes the patient, consistent practice of each part of an exercise for the pup to learn that she must do it *every* time you tell her. If you go too fast, you will only confuse her.

Remember the rare language dialect? Pronounce each word distinctly. "Sit," "stand," and "stay" are easily blurred beyond the pup's recognition. Put the *t* in "sitt." Emphasize the *t* and *a* in "sttaay," and put the *a-n-duh* in "st-and." Make "down" an upbeat word, not a growl (a broad smile helps).

Teaching "Drop It"

Use "drop it" when you want the pup to let go of a stolen or dangerous object. "Give it" may sound too much like "leave it," which could be confusing. "Drop it" has another advantage—you can say it so it sounds more like a growl (*"drrr-oppit"*), which makes the command more emphatic. Or, when returning a ball for a repeat throw, sweeten it with a smile, or for that use "give it."

Tricks and Treats

When your puppy has learned some of these basics, you can practice by turning it all into fun. For example, put the puppy in a sit, then encourage some gym exercise with a series of down-sit-down-sit until it's time for a treat.

Or put her on a sit-stay and let her watch you hide a toy under the edge of a nearby chair. Keep her on a stay for a moment more, perhaps as you wonder out loud, "Where is Teddy?" Then give her the release and cue, "okay—find Teddy!" If she hasn't figured out what to do, help her look for it. "Find it" becomes the command to locate any hidden item—and a good game.

> ### TIP
>
> **Good Timing**
>
> You may have noticed how the word "as" appears in everything you do in teaching your new puppy. Your puppy connects her action with your word command *only* at the precise instant they come together. Timing is vital. *What* you say is only as effective as *when* you say it. When you give a puppy a command as she just happens to be doing it on her own, your timing is perfect.

Keeping in mind the "*as*" timing explained in the box to the left, you can teach your puppy almost any trick simply by giving that action a one-word command. (Don't worry if it's actually two words; say them as one.) Dogs like to roll over onto their backs and wriggle, especially on a nice thick rug! Turn this back-scratching into a trick by catching Mimi *as* she begins and saying, "Mimi, roll over. Good girl!"

When Mimi has reached the stage of being able to hold a steady sit-stay, you can add another trick. Balance a small dog biscuit on top of her nose as you say "on trust." (You may have to hold her chin steady the first few times.) When she has held it for a second or two, give her the release signal ("okay" or "take it") *as* you gently but quickly lift her chin up, which will toss the biscuit into the air so she can catch the biscuit as it falls.

Kids and puppies love to play hide-and-seek, but anyone can get in on the game. Dogs seek by scent, so at least in the beginning crouch down to be nearer the pup's level. Put your puppy on a sit-stay, let her see you hide (behind a chair or a door) and then call out "find me!" Be sure she finds you, even if it means you have to call out her name a couple of times. Make a big deal of it when she does—and then repeat the game. Don't make it any more difficult until she can find you instantly at the easier level.

Reward her occasionally with a small treat, but make finding you the most exciting part of the game, which means you will progress slowly from hiding where she can at least partially see you to hiding in another room and eventually

A fun trick is to teach your dog the names of each of her toys, and to bring you only the toy you ask for.

the back of a clothes closet where your scent will be masked. She won't play if it isn't fun, so be sure she does find you every time.

Shaking hands is an old favorite and easy to teach—touch their toes and most pups will raise that paw. Lift it gently and say "shake hands" (or "give me a paw") *as* she does. When that much has been mastered, you can turn it into a paw raised higher, and without shaking it say "wave goodbye!" But that's for later; a polite puppy handshake is fine for now.

An alternative to using "off" to control jumping up is two paws raised in a jump-up greeting, but *only* on a command of "high five!"

There are plenty of games to play outdoors—mostly chasing toys or navigating obstacles. The "puppy pen" can contain all kinds of things as long as they are safe to chew, close to the ground, and can be kept relatively clean.

There's no such thing as failure in puppy games. Some dogs are naturally better than others at games in general. Some enjoy one type of game more than another. Go with your pup's game preferences now and you can expand them into tricks later. Don't be a pushy parent. Keep learning fun for both of you.

Chapter 9

Family Fun and Activities

When your puppy has had his immunizations, is mastering his obedience (or at least is beginning to behave nicely), and has matured mentally and physically, there will be loads of things you can do as a family with Rufus in tow. Sometimes he will be going along with you, at other times the trip will be especially for him.

There are some general rules when you take Rufus away from home. The first one is safety, so be sure his collar and leash are in good condition and the means of doggy transportation is secure. It seems everyone goes everywhere today with bottled water, so don't forget water for the dog! (Fill a bottle for him with water from home.) Restaurants in the United States are not canine-friendly, so keep in mind that your puppy may have to stay in the car while you eat. This is okay on a cool day, but heatstroke can occur on a merely warm day, and can be fatal. Plan a picnic instead!

Travels With Puppy

Visiting your family and friends means keeping a constant watch on the puppy. Unknown people and an unfamiliar environment may cause Rufus to forget his manners. If it's an overnight (or longer) visit, taking the dog's crate is essential—for him, for you, and for those nice people you're visiting. Also take enough food, water, bowls, treats, toys, and plastic clean-up bags to last your stay.

Hotels, motels, and bed-and-breakfasts do not all take kindly to canine guests. Some do not allow any pets, some allow only small ones, and some have an extra charge. Don't try to hide the dog! Find out the terms before making reservations.

If you really want to have family fun with the dog, look into the places that are specifically set up to welcome all of you. Many are in the country with facilities nearby for hiking, swimming, or sightseeing—with Rufus. As always, you are responsible for your dog's good behavior and for picking up after him.

Car Travel

Some dogs get carsick, and if Rufus does, before resorting to medication, try this. Put him where he will be safe in the car—in a crate, behind a barrier, or with a seat belt. Sit with him in the parked car, turn on the radio, read a magazine, or resort to cheerful chatter if you like, just to pass the time until he calms down. Take him out of the car and give him some playtime. The end of the first lesson.

The next time you turn on the engine, stay parked—and do it all over again. When he accepts that, move to step three—drive to the end of your driveway or a short distance down the street, park, get out and play, or go for a short walk. All's well? Go on to the fourth lesson. Drive to the nearest spot for a fun walk. Be certain he is okay with each lesson before going on to the next. And if none of this works, contact your vet.

For all trips, confine the dog to his crate, behind a barrier in the rear of the car, or use a canine seat belt. Never let a dog of any age put his head out the window of a car. Road dirt causes severe eye injury. (Very painful and very expensive to treat!)

Air Travel

Very small dogs may travel in the cabin of the plane if they fit in a crate tucked under the seat. All others travel in cargo. Airlines regulations change rather frequently, but the major rules do not.

Dogs are not accepted in extreme weather (cold or hot), and they must be in crates deemed safe and acceptable for air travel. Travel out of the country requires a veterinarian's health certificate, with additional regulations depending on your destination. Periods of quarantine are still enforced in many places. Check it all out *very carefully* when booking your flight, and follow the rules to the letter. These restrictions are law and there are no exceptions.

Boats

Here's a fun thing for everyone! Dogs very seldom get seasick and the only extras you'll need to take with you are a canine life preserver and towels for drying off a sea-sprayed dog. A leash is a must, and if you're going to be onboard a pleasure craft for any length of time, so is a designated "go potty" place. (Don't forget the paper towels and clean-up bags!)

Canoes are not the best choice for puppy antics afloat, but might be possible if Rufus can do a long sit-stay. A rowboat will allow even a large dog some fun time with you on the water. The life preserver will give you peace of mind should Rufus decide to jump ship.

Stay-at-Home Dog

Sometimes the dog has to stay home and either go to a boarding kennel or stay with a pet sitter. Be prepared to leave detailed instructions (you'll find a pet sitter checklist on page 7). The kennel will require a health certificate from the vet giving dates of immunizations, and a supply of food (and treats) if they do not feed what your puppy is fed, plus toys. Some even allow you to bring the puppy's own bed. Rufus may be given extra playtime for a small additional fee.

Your family will enjoy your dog more when you make him part of your family.

Grooming services may be available. Check it all out when you make your initial visit and inspection of the premises.

Canine Activities

Your playful puppy needs ways to burn off his excess energy. Even as an adult, regular exercise of both his mind and his body will keep him healthy and help maintain his good behavior.

Doggy Paddle

Dogs are not born knowing how to swim. In fact, many hate having to go out in the rain, to say nothing of tolerating a bath. But if you have a pool or live by water, teaching your puppy to swim is a *must*. This is a sport for dogs 6 months or older, because younger puppies lack coordination and may panic when their feet leave the ground. Puppies and adult dogs drown just as easily as any other land animal.

First check to be sure there is a safe, easy way for the dog to get *out* of a pool or pond (not up a ladder or through two feet of boggy mud). Coax the puppy to walk in with you, or carry him to where his feet are just off the ground and he begins to dog paddle. Then, with one arm around his body and your hand under his chest, gently lead him back to where his feet will touch bottom. Do not let go. Guide him to the chosen exit and show him how to get to solid ground or navigate a ramp. Towel dry him (most pups love that part). The end of the first lesson!

Each day extend the swim time only as long as your puppy is still enjoying it, or at least as long as he's not panic-stricken. Guard your dog as you would an eighteen-month-old baby! *Never* let him have access to a pool or pond unless an adult is not only with him, but is able to watch him even when he's not in the water. Kids mean well, but they should not be given total responsibility. When the dog is older (next summer, perhaps), he'll have enough savvy to go in with the kids. Provide shade, water, and a towel for a poolside pup. Yes, there are indeed poolside cabanas for dogs!

Hiking

Lots of dog owners are into outdoor activities, and hiking ranks high on the list. When your dog is physically mature enough to walk one mile a day, you can consider a brief hike. Have your vet check your pup's bone and muscle development to be sure your dog is ready for such exercise.

Start with a one-mile trek on an easy trail, and build up the distance and difficulty of the terrain very gradually. If you walk a mile in, remember you'll have to walk another mile out! Keep it short, family fun for starters, with lots of time for Rufus to sniff and investigate the new area. Most state, county, and town parks provide well-marked trails.

Whether you are hiking in the woods, the desert, a park, or along the shore, keep the dog on leash with proper ID and rabies tag on his collar. Remember your manners and move Rufus off the path to let others pass. A lack of common courtesy such as this has forced many areas to prohibit dogs.

An adult dog can wear a backpack (especially made for dogs) and help carry some of the things you'll need: water, bowl, treats, clean-up bags, an extra collar and leash, and a modified canine first-aid kit. For added safety, in case you or Rufus get lost, take along the vet's name, address, and phone number; a clear, close-up color photo of the dog; and a cell phone.

Agility and Obedience

These canine sports are a part of many all-breed dog shows. Agility is rather like an equestrian event, except that you don't get to ride a horse. You have to *run* an obstacle course alongside your dog. The newest event is rally-obedience, which is a bit confusing at first for the person, but more casual and interesting for the dog than the precision drills of regular obedience. You read signs telling you what you and Rufus are supposed to do, and you can chat with him all the way.

Carefully control introductions with dogs you do not know. Just because your pup is friendly and well-behaved doesn't mean every dog is.

Agility is a great favorite among dogs, but skip the jumps until your puppy is just about full grown, to avoid damage to growing bones.

All are fun to watch (the dogs are truly amazing), and fun to do with your puppy, whether or not you become involved in competition.

Breed-Specific Events

There are many breed-specific performance events that can be introduced at a puppy level. Contact local dog clubs for information on puppy training. Lure coursing is fun for sighthounds (such as Greyhounds and Whippets) and most other breeds. Fetching suitable objects on land or water is great for retrievers. Go-to-ground for all the small terrier breeds is easily accomplished using cartons opened at both ends to form a tunnel.

These are events that are designed to tap into the skills your dog was bred for. As adults, those puppy games are turned into competition events. Beagles go "beagling" (hunting in packs). Herding breeds have sheep herding tests. Hunting dogs have hunt tests and trials. There are races for sled dogs if you're into winter sports. And almost any dog can take up tracking.

All these events are generally free to spectators, you meet friendly people (all of whom are interested in the dogs and what they can do), and it's good family fun to watch and dream of how Rufus might perform. Of course, you may be smitten by the activity and become involved yourself.

Dog Parks

Dog parks are sprouting up in urban and suburban areas all over the country. All are set up to allow dogs to run and play off leash. That may sound like doggy heaven, but it has a downside. If aggressive dogs (or irresponsible owners) come in, there is the distinct probability a dogfight will ensue. Rules of etiquette are posted at the entrance, but as we know, some dogs can't read!

The dog park is not the place to go with a young puppy, no matter how inviting it may seem. Adult canine play and roughhousing is more than a puppy can cope with, either mentally or physically. Even when your puppy seems old enough, it's wise to keep his leash on for the first few visits, until you have evaluated the behavior of other dogs in the park (and their owners)—and to determine how Rufus reacts to it all.

There are health issues, too. An older dog won't be seriously affected picking up fleas or worms, but a puppy could be.

Appendix

Learning More About Your Puppy

Some Good Books

Training and Behavior

American Kennel Club, *The Complete Dog Book*, 19th edition, Revised, Howell Book House, 1998.

Arden, Andrea, *Dog Friendly Dog Training*, Howell Book House, 2000.

Benjamin, Carol Lea, *Mother Knows Best: The Natural Way to Train Your Dog*, Howell Book House, 1985.

Bonham, Margaret, *Introduction to Dog Agility*, Barron's, 2000.

Dunbar, Ian, *Dr. Dunbar's Good Little Dog Book*, James & Kenneth Publishers, 2003.

Kilcommons, Brian, and Sarah Wilson, *Good Owners, Great Dogs*, Warner Books, 1999.

Ryan, Terry, and Theresa Shipp, *The Ultimate Puppy*, Howell Book House, 2001.

Health Care and Nutrition

Giffin, James, MD, and Lisa Carlson, DVM, *The Dog Owner's Home Veterinary Handbook*, 3rd edition, Howell Book House, 1999.

Volhard, Wendy, and Kerry Brown, DVM, *Holistic Guide for a Healthy Dog*, 2nd edition, Howell Book House, 2000.

Wulff-Tilford, Mary L., *Herbs for Pets*, Bowtie Press, 1999.

Zink, Chris, *Dog Health & Nutrition for Dummies*, Hungry Minds, 2001.

Canine Art and Literature

Albert, Fred, *Barkitecture,* Abbeville Press, 1999.

Eichorn, Gary E., *The Dog Album: Studio Portraits of People and Their Dogs,* Stewart, Tabori & Chang, 2000.

Rowan, Roy, and Brooke Janis, *First Dogs: American Presidents and Their Best Friends,* Workman Publishing, 1997.

Secord, William, A *Breed Apart: The Art Collections of the American Kennel Club and the AKC Museum of the Dog,* Antique Collectors' Club, 2001.

Shaff, Valerie, *I am Puppy, Hear Me Yap!,* HarperCollins Publishers, 2000.

Stifel, William F., *The Dog Show—125 Years of Westminster,* Westminster Kennel Club, 2001.

Zaczek, Iain, *Dog: A Dog's Life in Art and Literature,* Watson-Guptill, 2000.

Magazines

AKC Gazette
AKC Family Dog
260 Madison Ave.
New York, NY 10016
(800) 533-7323
www.akc.org

The Bark
2810 8th St.
Berkeley, CA 94710
(877) BARKNEWS
www.thebark.com

Dog & Kennel
Pet Publishing, Inc.
7-L Dundas Circle
Greensboro, NC 27407
(336) 292-4047
www.dogandkennel.com

Dog Fancy
Dog World
3 Burroughs
Irvine, CA 92618
(949) 855-8822
www.dogfancy.com
www.dogworldmag.com

Videos

Sirius Puppy Training
Ian Dunbar provides new puppy owners with an array of easy techniques to train their dogs. Learn how to establish a bond with your puppy, how to get off-leash control, and how to teach simple commands. The ninety-minute video also includes important information on problem prevention and training.
Available from the DogWise catalog for $29.95
(800) 776-2665
www.dogwise.com

Puppy Love: Raise Your Dog the Clicker Way
Clicker-training guru Karen Pryor shows you the gentle way to train your puppy in this thirty-minute video. Teach all the basics with the click of a clicker.
Available from the DogWise catalog for $24.95
(800) 776-2665
www.dogwise.com

Sarah's PuppyPerfect Video
Get your whole family involved as this cheerful video covers all aspects of puppyhood, from buying the right equipment to puppy training and problem solving.
Available from Simply Sarah Inc for $24.95
www.dogperfect.com

Canine Registries

American Kennel Club
260 Madison Avenue, 4th Floor
New York, NY 10016
(212) 696-8200
www.akc.org

United Kennel Club
100 E. Kilgore Road
Kalamazoo, MI 49001-5598
(616) 343-9020
www.ukcdogs.com

American Rare Breed Association
9921 Frank Tippet Road
Cheltenham, MD 20612
(301) 868-5718
www.arba.org

Canadian Kennel Club
89 Skyway Avenue
Etobicoke, Ontario
Canada M9W 6R4
(800) 250-8040, (416) 675-5511
www.ckc.ca

Health Resources

AKC Canine Health Foundation
251 W. Garfield Road, Suite 160
Aurora, OH 44202
(888) 682-9696
www.akcchf.org or www.caninehealthonline.org

Canine Eye Registry Foundation (CERF)
Veterinary Medical Data Base
Purdue University
625 Harrison Street
West Lafayette, IN 47907
(765) 494-8179
vmdb@vmdb.org

Orthopedic Foundation for Animals (OFA)
2300 E. Nifong Boulevard
Columbia, MO 65201-3856
(573) 442-0418
www.ofa.org

University of Pennsylvania Hip Improvement Program (PennHIP)
University of Pennsylvania School of Veterinary Medicine
3900 Delancey Street
Philadelphia, PA 19104-6010
(215) 573-3176
www.pennhip.org

Helpful Web Sites

American Boarding Kennel Association
www.abka.com
A nonprofit association setting high standards for the pet boarding industry. Log on for a complete list of member kennels (internationally), and tips on how to select the right one for you and your dog.

American Kennel Club
www.akc.org
Visit the AKC's web site for in-depth information on all recognized dog breeds, including breed standards. The site provides links to dog breed clubs and rescue groups around the country.

Canine Medicine Chest
www.caninemedicinechest.com
This site offers extensive information for the pet owner seeking holistic remedies for their dog. It also offers a free consultation at (712) 644-3535.

Cyber-Dog
www.cyberpet.com/cyberdog/
If you want to be entertained and informed at the same time, visit this site. A helmeted Cyber Dog will escort you on a journey through all areas of cyberspace that pertain to pooches.

Dog Breed Info Center
www.dogbreedinfo.com
All dog lovers should visit this information-packed site. Log on to learn more about specific dog breeds, find out details about canine health, and learn to customize a mouse pad with your puppy's picture.

InfoDog

www.infodog.com

If you are interested in dog shows and events—including obedience and agility—look no further. This web site contains an extensive list of national and local dog shows, photographs of show winners, and links to sites of interest to dog fanciers.

The National Dog Rescue Connection

members.tripod.com/ndrc/index.htm

Stop by this web site if you have your heart set on rescuing or adopting a dog. There are links to adoption sites and suggestions for how you can contribute to canine welfare groups.

Pets on the Go

www.petsonthego.com

Dawn and Robert Habgood were pioneers in making any vacation with our dogs a pleasure. Their web site gives in-depth descriptions of hotels, motels, inns, and B&Bs where your dog will be treated like an honored guest. Included are suggestions for sightseeing and things to do with your dog once you get there.

Spay USA

www.spayusa.org

The world's largest low-cost spay-neuter referral program, with more than 900 participants nationwide. The site includes information on why you should spay or neuter your pet. You can also call 1-888-PETS-911 or 1-800-248-SPAY to locate a low-cost facility near you.

Vet Info.com

www.vetinfo.com/dogindex.html

Visit this comprehensive web site for information on dog ailments and health. Diseases and conditions are listed in alphabetical order.

Photo Credits:

Kent Dannen: 1, 8–9, 12, 25, 28, 30, 31, 33, 41, 42, 44–45, 47, 50, 55, 59, 65, 68, 76, 82, 94, 87, 89, 98, 99 (top), 103, 119, 121, 123, 124, 128, 130, 132, 133

Mary Bloom: 11, 13, 22, 23, 34, 35, 39, 46, 52, 54, 57, 61, 63 (top), 64, 69, 73, 74, 85, 90, 92, 96–97, 99 (bottom), 100, 104, 105, 107, 108, 110, 113, 116

Jeannie Harrison: 16, 17, 20, 37, 60, 63 (bottom), 75, 77, 114, 127

Index